THE COBAD SYNDROME

New Hope for People Suffering from the
Inherited Syndrome of
Childhood-Onset Bipolar Disorder with ADHD

by
WILLIAM NIEDERHUT, M.D.

authorHOUSE™

1663 Liberty Drive, Suite 200
Bloomington, Indiana 47403
(800) 839-8640
www.AuthorHouse.com

First published by AuthorHouse 07/07/05

ISBN: 1-4208-6701-6 (sc)

Library of Congress Control Number: 2005905740

Printed in the United States of America
Bloomington, Indiana

This book is printed on acid-free paper.

for Elisabeth and Katherine

Contents

Acknowledgements

This book was written for people everywhere who are suffering from the COBAD syndrome--childhood-onset bipolar disorder with ADHD--and for the doctors, therapists, and family members who are trying to help them. Much of the data in the book has come from the excellent research of Dr. Joseph Biederman and his colleagues – Drs. Janet Wozniak, Stephen Faraone, Timothy Wilens, and others – at the Pediatric Psychopharmacology Clinic of the Massachusetts General Hospital. A great deal has also come from the many adult patients in my practice who I have had the privilege to work with during the past decade. I am very grateful to all of them for their patience with my own shortcomings, and their willingness to teach me much of what I know about the COBAD syndrome. I also appreciate their permission to discuss details of their case histories in this book. I have presented these case histories in a disguised form in order to protect their privacy, while preserving the essential psychiatric details.

I am also especially grateful to my wife, Dr. Diane Lehman, for her many helpful comments and major editorial assistance in the preparation of this manuscript. She has been so much more than a best friend and life partner, despite the many trials and tribulations that we have endured as the parents of two disabled children. Words cannot express the love and gratitude that I feel for her for all that she has done for me and for our daughters.

W.N.

Chapter 1

The Most Beautiful Girls in the World

Just after midnight on January 16, 1994 my life changed forever. After several tense hours in a hospital delivery room our obstetrician decided that a Caesarian section was necessary. My wife was wheeled into an operating room and placed under the bright lights. Standing behind the doctors and nurses at the table I lost all sense of time. Did an hour pass? A few minutes? I saw them draw a tiny red mass from my wife's belly toward the lights. There was a strange, unpregnant silence. Then, after what seemed like an eternity, I heard a faint cry. A nurse washed the baby and held her out to me. She was more precious than any jewel, and so tiny! I had never held such a treasure. We had almost lost this girl six months into the pregnancy when my wife went into premature labor, and now she was here, in my arms, alive! I heard someone telling me to take my daughter down the hall to the nursery while my wife rested in the recovery room. I was walking on air all the way down the deserted neon-lit corridor. My daughter had her tiny hand wrapped tightly around my little finger, and I thought: "I'll always be here for you, kid." She was the most beautiful girl in the world.

I could scarcely have imagined on that special night so many years ago the tragedy that lay ahead of us. It was to unfold in a series of discoveries, progressively more bewildering and painful for all of us. At times things became almost unbearable, and my wife and I went about our daily lives in quiet--and, sometimes, not so quiet--desperation, feeling increasingly isolated from our family, community, and few remaining friends. We both became obsessed with understanding the nature of this tragedy, searching through medical journals and books for answers. I looked deeply into the history of my own family, and my life, for clues. Gradually, this searching led to a clearer understanding of my family pathology, and that of others, but it was not an understanding that I found readily in medical journals or books. I realized that I was discovering something in myself and in my adult patients that had not even been clearly *named* by modern medicine. I was also to discover in my work as a psychiatrist that this unnamed syndrome could be effectively treated in many of my adult patients, and that something of value could come from our personal travail.

My daughter was a lovely, vivacious toddler. She was partially deaf at birth, but, like most children, had a vivid imagination and loved to hear stories. I often made up stories for her, like one about seven princesses from seven kingdoms, each with her own accoutrements of precious stones: diamonds, rubies, emeralds, sapphires, or amethysts. She began to write her own stories at an early age, and read them with panache. When she was eight years old she won a poetry contest sponsored by a prominent bookstore in our city, and I had fantasies of my daughter growing up to become a great writer, perhaps going to Harvard as I had done, helping humanity. I was not overly worried when, at age five, she began to sit in the back of her kindergarten classroom, complaining that the other children in the class had "bad breath." Hadn't I also always been somewhat aloof, a maverick? She seemed depressed at age two after her sister was born, but wasn't that natural? No one is happy about being displaced by a younger sibling. When she began to have severe temper tantrums at age two, I also attributed them to sibling

2

rivalry. Her fits of rage and extreme sensitivity to minor offenses reminded me of my own sisters.

Then, on a balmy October evening during her second grade year, I was sitting outdoors after dinner enjoying the fall colors of the garden. My oldest daughter and I were chatting about school. Her teacher had called earlier in the day to tell us that she had written a note to a boy in her class that said: "I hate you." It seemed out of character for her because she was, despite the occasional temper tantrums, a kind, sensitive girl. As I questioned her, she told me that some of her classmates were "evil" and others were "good." The evil ones were leprechauns, including a boy named Ivan who was trying to kill her with his "special powers." The good ones, like her friend Zoe, were fairies who could cast protective spells. I had not been around young children much in my adult years, but certainly wondered about what sounded more like psychosis than mere imagination. Finally, as we talked, my daughter told me, reluctantly, that she had actually *seen* Ivan standing in her room one night threatening to kill her with a knife. I consulted a textbook of child psychiatry and felt somewhat reassured by a comment that "hallucinations in childhood"--especially those occurring around bedtime, called hypnogogic and hypnopompic--"should not be a cause for undue alarm." It didn't take much to convince me at the time that nothing was seriously wrong. Who wants to believe that their child has a serious mental illness?

It took a few more weeks, and a greater shock, for my wife and I to finally overcome our denial and consult a child psychiatrist. In retrospect, I can see that part of the problem was that, for the longest time, I had been comparing my oldest daughter's experiences to my own, as if *I* had been a normal child from a normal family! In fact, I had always been *different*; a nonconformist who had trouble thinking *inside* of the box, and my daughter had her own, peculiar way of looking at the world. She had also never been able to sleep very well, and I had memories of lying awake most of the night as a child. I hated taking naps during childhood, and so did my daughter. In fact, she got into trouble at daycare when she was three years old for refusing to take a nap and wandering around the building to the superintendent's office. I thought that this was somewhat amusing, and recalled being sent to the principal's office in kindergarten for jumping out of an invitingly open classroom window! She had been experiencing temper tantrums and crying jags since early childhood which I misconstrued as normal because they seemed so familiar from my own childhood. Then one night in December, as I was decorating the house for the holidays, my daughter started talking animatedly to the Christmas tree. Even *I* had never done that.

My greatest fear that Christmas was that my daughter might be suffering from childhood schizophrenia. She was seeing and hearing things and, as I discovered, had developed delusional ideas based upon her hallucinations. Her stuffed animals had been talking to her and even conspiring against her. She had also become socially withdrawn and preoccupied with writing cryptic "plays" that were disorganized and virtually impossible to understand. But my wife, a child psychologist, thought that she might be bipolar. She had been studying the newly emerging literature about bipolar disorders in childhood and was impressed by our daughter's intense moodiness and lifelong sleep problems. She also knew that schizophrenia is extremely rare in children, and that there was no history of schizophrenia in our families.

At the time I didn't think that *I* was bipolar. I am a psychiatrist and had been working with bipolar adults for many years. I knew that I had been depressed at times, probably since childhood, and I had taken an antidepressant called desipramine for almost ten years in the past. Tricyclic antidepressants like desipramine were known to cause mood swings and mania in bipolar people, and if I were bipolar, I reasoned, desipramine would have probably induced symptoms of hypomania during a ten-year period: insomnia, irritability, racing thoughts, and bursts of goal-directed activity. In contrast, during my ten years on desipramine, I had felt just the opposite: calm, cool, and collected, almost to a fault. I had spent my time working long hours, and had not experienced the occasional bursts of creative energy and irritability that I had known in my youth.

The child psychiatrist that we saw that December started our daughter on the antipsychotic medication Risperdal, and we gradually raised the dose higher and higher in an attempt to control her hallucinations. She *did* become less irritable, and less tormented by hallucinations and fear, but her ability to read and function at school became progressively worse. Instead of writing colorful poems she spent hours brooding over an empty journal, unable to scribble more than a few sentences. When we tried to reduce the Risperdal dose she became even more withdrawn and confused. Finally, in February of that year, my wife and I attended a lecture on childhood bipolar disorders by the Harvard psychiatrist Dr. Joseph Biederman, and felt somewhat reassured that a study from his clinic at the Massachusetts General Hospital had shown that Risperdal probably worked better than anything to control mood swings in bipolar children. Since it was also effective in schizophrenia, it seemed an optimal choice for my daughter, regardless of the possible bipolar diagnosis. In his lecture Dr. Biederman also mentioned the findings from his clinic that most bipolar children have attention deficit hyperactivity disorder (ADHD), but I failed to appreciate the significance of that information at the time. I was still trying to determine whether my daughter had a bipolar disorder or a rare type of schizophrenia, and which treatment might be best for her. She had been born prematurely and had also been exposed in utero to magnesium sulfate, terbutaline, and steroids in an attempt to prevent pre-term labor and accelerate her lung maturation. Was she suffering from prenatal brain damage? An MRI scan had shown a cyst near the tegmentum of her brain, and a neurosurgeon had speculated that it might, conceivably, be the cause of her hallucinations.

Then, two years after our oldest daughter became ill, something equally terrible happened. Our youngest daughter--a beautiful, intelligent child who was well liked by her classmates and teachers--became severely depressed, anxious, and irritable. She also stopped reading books, and became withdrawn and confused at school. When her teacher asked her to solve a simple math problem one day she had burst into tears, complaining that she couldn't think. A few weeks later we were watching a DVD of the Steven Sondheim musical, Into the Woods, in our living room, and my youngest daughter became very frightened. She began to experience visual hallucinations of giant wolves in our house, and had delusions that they were conspiring to kill her. We took her to see the child psychiatrist treating our oldest daughter and she was also started on Risperdal. Her hallucinations and delusions gradually went away during the next few weeks. However, she, like her sister, also experienced a marked deterioration in her cognitive functioning and school performance, and eventually stopped reading altogether. My wife and I noticed, in our grief, that the age at onset of her symptoms, five years, was eerily similar to that of her sister. Unlike her sister, however, my youngest daughter's birth had been free of any complications. So what, I

6

asked myself, was destroying her mind? What was this mental illness of childhood that was destroying both of my beautiful, innocent daughters, and where did it come from? I became obsessed with these questions. Then slowly, all too slowly, I began to find the answers. In the meantime, it was all I could do, literally, to keep the wolves from our door.

Chapter 2

Bipolar Disorders

In the nineteenth century the French physician Pierre Janet used the term "folie circulaire," or "circular psychosis," to describe mental patients suffering from *episodic* bouts of insanity. The German psychiatrist Emil Kraepelin, whose observations became the basis for much of our modern *Diagnostic and Statistical Manual of Mental Disorders*, used the term "maniacal-depressive insanity" to describe similar patients he had treated in asylums at Heidelberg and Munich. In his lectures and textbooks Kraepelin presented vivid descriptions of such patients as a basis for diagnosis and *prognosis*, the prediction of the future course of the illness. Kraepelin's term "manic-depression" referred to the biphasic, or *bipolar*, course of the illness, since the patients suffered from episodes of both depression--despair, apathy, and fatigue--and mania. When manic they felt elated or extremely irritable, with increased energy, talkativeness, and ambition. They often--like one young merchant under Kraepelin's care-- engaged in sexual indiscretions and embarked on reckless business ventures on such occasions, only to end up in the asylum later in a severely depressed, apathetic state. When manic, they sometimes experienced hallucinations and delusional ideas of reality, often centered on grandiose or religious themes. During the depressive episodes they tended to have unrealistically gloomy perceptions of themselves and the world around them. Kraepelin made a special point of differentiating his manic-depressive patients from those with "dementia praecox," who had a more insidious course of illness, characterized by persistent hallucinations and delusional ideas which occurred independently of changes in mood and volition. The Swiss psychiatrist Eugen Bleuler later coined the term "schizophrenia," to denote what Kraepelin had called dementia praecox.

Unfortunately, much of Kraepelin's precise, descriptive work was neglected by psychiatrists for almost a century. In the history of psychiatry, as of medicine generally, paradigms of diagnosis have often evolved in relation to effective treatment options. His "descriptive psychiatry" was useful for prognostication, but offered little in the way of effective treatment. Descriptive psychiatrists at the turn of the century, including Eugen Bleuler and Carl Jung of the highly regarded "Zurich school," became understandably interested in the emerging "interpretive psychiatry" of psychoanalysis, as did their American colleagues. Sigmund Freud's psychoanalytic discoveries and theories offered new hope for therapeutic efficacy and were eagerly applied to the general theory and practice of psychiatry. This general "interpretive," psychoanalytic approach prevailed in American psychiatry for almost eighty years, and is still prevalent in much of our thinking about the nature and treatment of mental illnesses. For example, when I ask people today about their history of depressive symptoms they will usually begin with an "interpretive" explanation rather than a description. They often say something like: "I felt very depressed last November *because* my friend moved to Seattle," rather than saying: "I have noticed a pattern of feeling depressed and sleeping a lot every year beginning in November." This psychoanalytic, interpretive tendency has been so paradigmatic in our modern culture that many people are still quite resistant to the idea of taking a medication to correct biologically based problems of mood, sleep, attention, or thought.

In the 1950's, a number of drugs were found to dramatically improve symptoms of many common mental illnesses, and the interpretive psychoanalytic paradigms began to be questioned. Thorazine was found to reduce hallucinations and paranoia in people suffering from schizophrenia, and iproniazid, developed as a treatment for tuberculosis, was found to improve symptoms of depression. The first tricyclic antidepressant, imipramine, was discovered in Switzerland in the 1950's as a derivative of an antihistamine. In a major breakthrough for people with manic-depression, lithium salt was found in 1949 to control the mood swings seen in manic-depression. Unfortunately, the FDA did not authorize the use of lithium in the United States until 1970, mainly because--being a natural, elemental substance--it could not be patented, and pharmaceutical companies had no incentive to finance its authorization by the FDA. American psychiatrists were, consequently, slow to routinely diagnose and treat manic-depression. As an example of this, I recall working as a psychiatric resident at a busy city hospital in 1985 with many patients suffering from manic-depression. In reviewing their hospital records from the 1960's and 70's, I noticed that almost all of these patients had been previously diagnosed with "schizophrenia," even though their histories showed episodic depression and mania, as Kraepelin had described in his manic-depressive patients a century earlier. They were clearly manic-depressive, or--as the *Diagnostic and Statistical Manual of Mental Disorders III* of American psychiatry, published in 1980, so poetically described them--"bipolar."

During the past twenty years, the improved recognition and treatment of bipolar disorders has been a major achievement of American psychiatry. One important concept that has emerged from a careful review of Kraepelin's work, and from modern epidemiological research by Dr. Hagop Akiskal and others, is that bipolar disorders occur in a "spectrum" of severity. We now know that not all people suffering from bipolar disorders experience the severe manic-depressive cycles described over a century ago by Kraepelin. Many suffer mainly from episodes of recurrent or protracted depression without obvious mania. On careful review, they may have experienced episodes of agitation and mild mania, called "hypomania," either spontaneously or while taking commonly prescribed antidepressant medications. Others, perhaps as many as one third of all bipolar people, suffer from *mixed* symptoms of simultaneous depression and manic agitation, and are classified as "bipolar, mixed." (Kraepelin had, in fact, described cases of "mixed" bipolar disorders in his lectures.) Bipolar people with multiple mood cycles per year have been further classified as "rapid-cyclers." Other syndromes in the bipolar spectrum are "cyclothymia," and "hyperthymic temperament," referring to people who are typically energetic, outgoing, and creative: often, in the case of cyclothymia, with episodic bouts of mild depression.

The *essential* diagnostic feature of any bipolar disorder is a history of *hypomania* or mania. When hypomanic, people experience episodes of *elation or irritability with increased energy, a reduced need for sleep, accelerated thought and speech, and intense goal-directed activity.* When manic, they experience such symptoms in a more severe, persistent form, typically for at least one week. A useful screening test for hypomania, called the Mood Disorder Questionnaire (MDQ), is shown in Chapter 9, and should be reviewed by anyone suffering from depression. The current *Diagnostic and Statistical Manual of Mental Disorders (DSM-IV)* diagnostic criteria for hypomania, and for the depressed phases seen in bipolar disorders--major depression and dysthymia-- are listed below.

Diagnostic Criteria for Hypomania

A distinct period of persistently elevated, expansive, or irritable mood, lasting throughout at least 4 days, with three (or more) of the following symptoms (four if the mood is only irritable):

- inflated self-esteem or grandiosity
- decreased need for sleep
- more talkative than usual or pressure to keep talking
- flight of ideas or subjective experience that thoughts are racing
- distractibility
- increase in goal-directed activity or psychomotor agitation
- excessive involvement in pleasurable activities that have a high potential for painful consequences

---

Diagnostic Criteria for Major Depression

Five (or more) of the following symptoms have been present during the same 2-week period and at least one of the symptoms is either depressed mood or loss of interest or pleasure:

- depressed mood most of the day, nearly every day. (In children and adolescents, can be irritable mood.)
- markedly diminished interest or pleasure in all, or almost all, activities
- significant weight loss when not dieting or weight gain, or decrease or increase in appetite
- insomnia or hypersomnia
- psychomotor agitation or retardation nearly every day
- fatigue or loss of energy nearly every day
- feelings of worthlessness or excessive or inappropriate guilt
- diminished ability to think or concentrate, or indecisiveness
- recurrent thoughts of death or suicidal ideation

Diagnostic Criteria for Dysthymia

Depressed mood for most of the day, for more days than not for at least 2 years (in children and adolescents, mood can be irritable and duration must be at least 1 year) with two (or more) of the following:

- poor appetite or overeating
- insomnia or hypersomnia
- low energy or fatigue
- low self-esteem
- poor concentration or difficulty making decisions
- feelings of hopelessness

After Prozac came on the market, in 1988, psychiatrists and primary care physicians began to prescribe antidepressants on a much wider scale for people suffering from depressive symptoms. A number of SSRI's (an acronym for "selective serotonin reuptake inhibitors") similar to Prozac were produced in rapid succession in the 1990's--Zoloft, Paxil, Luvox, Celexa, and Lexapro--and there were heavy advertising campaigns directed at physicians and the public as each drug tried to carve out a "market share" by distinguishing itself from the others. Many people suffering from depression and anxiety disorders have benefited from these drugs, and they have done much to improve the public welfare on a grand scale.   Unfortunately, they have also often been prescribed inappropriately for people with undiagnosed *bipolar* disorders, a practice that may cause mood swings and hypomania. Psychiatrists have been very busy during the past decade treating hypomania and mania in bipolar patients who were started on antidepressants during an episode of depression. I still remember Charlie, a 50-year-old salesman, who I evaluated in the early 1990's at an alcohol treatment center. He had been drinking heavily for several months after his doctor had prescribed Prozac for an episode of depression. He had been unable to sleep after starting Prozac, and had embarked on a series of disastrous business ventures before being arrested for drunk and disorderly conduct at a local ski resort. When I asked him about his arrest, he told me that he had been soliciting potential customers for a portable golf ball driving range that he had built in the back of his pickup truck! Charlie ceased being a member of the "Prozac nation" after our initial meeting, and felt much better on lithium.

Psychiatric research has attempted to clarify which people suffering from depression, like Charlie, are likely to have hidden bipolar disorders. In the mid 1990's, for example, Dr. Akiskal and his colleagues published a series of important papers about depression and bipolar spectrum disorders as part of a large-scale study called the NIMH Collaborative Project on the Psychobiology of Depression. Among other things, they found that people who had experienced the onset of depression in *childhood or adolescence* often ended up having bipolar disorders. In another study, they followed a group of depressed adults during an eleven-year period to see which characteristics would predict future hypomania or mania. The results were important, and confirmed a discovery from a study published two years earlier by the American psychiatric epidemiologist Dr. George Winokur. The depressed adults who became hypomanic over time, but not fully manic--what is now called bipolar type II-- often had a history of *early-onset mood problems, persistent mood instability, a tendency to daydream, frequent job changes, and a high incidence of substance abuse.* It is now clear that many of the characteristics identified by Dr. Akiskal in these bipolar II adults are the same things seen in people with *ADHD*, though he did not refer to them in his study as ADHD symptoms. There was a reason for this omission. Dr. Akiskal, like most psychiatrists working with adults at that time, was not in the habit of diagnosing or treating ADHD. It was believed to be a disorder of childhood and adolescence that spontaneously resolved by adulthood.

Chapter 3

Attention-Deficit Disorder

In the summer of 1995, just when I thought that I had mastered all of the *essentials* of adult psychiatry, a new psychiatrist, Dr. William Dodson, moved into the office next to mine at the University of Colorado Health Sciences Center. He asked me to cover for his patients during a trip out of town shortly after his arrival, and I felt nervous when several of his adult patients called me that week asking for prescriptions for an amphetamine compound called Adderall. I had rarely prescribed amphetamines or other drugs of that class, called stimulants, during the previous ten years of my work in adult psychiatric hospitals and clinics. The only doctors I knew who prescribed them were either child psychiatrists treating children and adolescents with ADHD, or "quacks" treating obesity. Was Bill some sort of quack prescribing amphetamines for people who wanted to lose weight? I nervously wrote a few refills to get his patients through the week, and politely expressed my concerns when he returned to town. "They are being treated for ADHD," he explained. I was puzzled because I had been trained to think of ADHD as a disorder of childhood that resolved by age eighteen. Didn't I know all of the *essentials* of adult psychiatry? I had scored in the top one percent in the nation on my American Board of Psychiatry and Neurology examinations just a few years earlier.

A few weeks later I saw a nurse, Julie, who Bill had treated in our University Hospital ward. She was obviously bipolar, having suffered a series of crippling depressive episodes alternating with hypomania for several years. In the hospital Julie had undergone shock treatments, and was now taking a regimen of medications that Bill had prescribed, including mood stabilizers, the SSRI antidepressant Zoloft, and Adderall. As I nervously reviewed her history, I noticed that Bill had diagnosed *both* bipolar disorder and ADHD. Coincidentally, Julie had scheduled a consultation, while in the hospital, with our local psychiatric *guru*, a professor who is widely respected for his knowledge of psychiatry. In his report, the professor advised me to stop the Adderall and Zoloft as soon as possible, noting that Julie was exhibiting signs of hypomania. I saw her in my office after receiving the professor's letter and was determined to stop the "uppers." But before I could say a word, she sat down calmly and said: "This is the best I have ever felt in my life." I suspected that she was hypomanic, with "euphoria"--a high or elevated mood--and went through a checklist of symptoms of hypomania. It was negative. She was sleeping well. Her thoughts were not racing. She was not irritable or anxious. She was not feeling impulsive: wanting to spend money, argue, or noticing increased sex drive. She also told me that she felt more organized in her personal and work life than she had ever been, and was able to wake up feeling alert and awake for the first time in her life. Best of all, she was not depressed.

I was pleasantly surprised, but a little perplexed. I had learned through many years of trial and error that, when treating bipolar disorders, "if something isn't broken, don't fix it." There are so many unknowns, though doctors and patients are, as Martin Luther King once said about modern man, "uncomfortable with mystery." I had also learned to trust my observations, even if one of the "experts" disagreed with me. So I, cautiously, decided to disregard the *guru's* expert advice and keep Julie on Zoloft and Adderall. My wife and I spoke to the professor a few weeks later at a gala lecture he was presenting on bipolar disorders. "What do you make of this adult ADHD business?" I asked warily. "Is there something to the data about its prevalence beyond the adolescent years?" He seemed, as my wife recalls, a bit contemptuous when he said, "Hypomania can certainly be *misdiagnosed* as ADHD, and patients on *amphetamines* can certainly get hypomanic!" I would have been somewhat chagrined but I wasn't convinced that he was correct on this occasion. Julie hadn't *been* hypomanic, at least in my office.

The professor was not the only skeptic in our ranks. As Bill Dodson began to lecture about adult ADHD around the campus and community (and, later, around the country through his work for Shire Pharmaceuticals) there were grumblings from my own psychiatric circle at the University. We had all seen patients who had become hypomanic on stimulants. The dogma in American psychiatry at the time was that even *antidepressants* should not be used in the treatment of bipolar disorders, much less potent stimulants like amphetamines. Our caution was partly a response to the epidemic of hypomania and mania that had resulted from the widespread use of SSRI antidepressants several years earlier. But several of our group couldn't help being impressed by the positive responses that many of our patients with ADHD symptoms were having to stimulant trials. One of my colleagues, a psychoanalyst, remarked at a lunch meeting that he was amazed at the responses that several of his long-term, treatment-resistant depressed patients with ADHD had been having to stimulants. I noticed the same thing in my practice, and began to diagnose and treat ADHD more routinely in my adult patients. But I remained cautious about starting bipolar patients on stimulants for a long time. The first line of the Hippocratic oath is, "Primum non nocere." It is

Latin for, "First, do no harm," and I did not want to risk harming a bipolar patient by prescribing medications that might cause mania or psychosis.

Research during the past decade has, in fact, clarified a number of things about adult ADHD that were unclear to me and to most adult psychiatrists in 1995, and most psychiatrists treating adults are now actively diagnosing and treating ADHD. Unfortunately, many people, including some doctors, still question the validity of ADHD as a biologically based adult disorder. Some of these are the same people who still believe that the human brain is, in some way, invulnerable to the biochemical malfunctioning that afflicts the other organs of the human body. There is a persistent belief in our society that abnormal brain chemistry should not be corrected in the same way that we use medications to correct physiological problems like diabetes or high blood pressure. In truth, medications can be harmful if misused, like any technology, but there may also be harmful consequences to *not* using them appropriately. Untreated ADHD, for example, is associated with an increased risk of substance abuse, accidents, and poor outcomes in work, education, and personal relationships.

So, here are some basic scientific facts about ADHD. First, it is clear that many children have ADHD, from 3 to 10% of all children in various studies, and that about half continue to experience significant symptoms of ADHD in adulthood. Second, ADHD has been shown to be a biologically based disorder with strong genetic determinants. Third, ADHD can be very effectively treated in most children and adults with medications that increase dopamine and norepinephrine activity in the brain. The most effective of these are the stimulants: methylphenidate (Ritalin, Ritalin LA, Concerta), and amphetamine (Dexedrine, Adderall, and Adderall XR.) Other drugs which increase norepinephrine neurotransmission, such as desipramine, bupropion (Wellbutrin), atomoxetine (Strattera), and venlafaxine (Effexor) also improve ADHD symptoms, though their effects may be delayed and less pronounced. Psychotherapy, especially cognitive-behavioral therapy and skills training, is often helpful for people with ADHD, but does *not* result in a significant remission of ADHD symptoms in the absence of treatment with stimulant medication. This was demonstrated most convincingly in a large-scale NIMH funded study, the Multimodal Treatment Study of Children with ADHD (MTA), published in the *Archives of General Psychiatry* in 1999. Furthermore, brain scans (SPECT, PET, MRI) and quantitative electroencephalograms (qEEG) can be used to corroborate a diagnosis of ADHD, *but they do not significantly improve upon diagnosis by a careful history.* They are also expensive and, in the case of some brain scans which use radiation, potentially harmful.

To elaborate briefly on these basic facts about ADHD, I should mention that the syndrome of distractibility, hyperactivity, and impulsivity that we now call ADHD has been recognized in children for over a century. Young girls with ADHD have been under diagnosed, historically, because they suffer primarily from impaired attention, with less hyperactivity than boys. In 1937, Dr. Charles Bradley discovered that symptoms of inattention and hyperactivity in institutionalized boys with ADHD (called "minimal brain dysfunction" at the time) could be dramatically improved by stimulant medication. Since then, a great deal of controlled research has confirmed that distractibility, hyperactivity, and impulsivity in children with ADHD are improved by stimulants. In the 1970's some psychiatrists, notably Dr. Paul Wender, began to find that ADHD could be diagnosed in adults. Subsequent research has confirmed that ADHD is highly prevalent in adults, and can be effectively treated with the same medications that work for children with ADHD. Most adults with ADHD describe problems with inattention, and their childhood hyperactivity, if present, has usually diminished to a level of physical restlessness.

As mentioned above, research on ADHD has shown that there are strong genetic determinants, estimated at a very high 70-80%, for the disorder. These estimates are based on the analysis of families, twins, and adopted children with ADHD. About half of all children of a parent with ADHD also have ADHD, and 25% of parents of an ADHD child have ADHD. Although the molecular mechanism of ADHD has not been clearly delineated, studies have focused on the neurotransmitters norepinephrine and dopamine, which play an important role in the activation of prefrontal brain regions regulating attention, executive functioning, and impulse control. Functional Magnetic Resonance (fMRI) and Positron Emission (PET) scans have confirmed that people with ADHD have abnormalities of prefrontal brain circuits that serve executive functions. Some studies in children and adults with ADHD have also shown increased concentrations of dopamine, and of the dopamine transporter (DAT), in prefrontal brain circuitry. Molecular genetic studies of ADHD have implicated possible abnormalities in genes coding for the dopamine transporter (DAT) and the D4 and D5 dopamine receptors.

A useful screening test for adult ADHD developed by the World Health Organization, the Adult Self-Report Scale (ASRS), is shown in Chapter 9. The *DSM-IV* diagnostic criteria for ADHD are listed below.

Symptoms of
Attention-Deficit/Hyperactivity Disorder

Six (or more) of the symptoms listed under either inattention or hyperactivity-impulsivity:

Inattention:

- often fails to give close attention to details or makes careless mistakes in schoolwork, work, or other activities
- often has difficulty sustaining attention in tasks or play activities
- often does not seem to listen when spoken to directly
- often does not follow through on instructions and fails to finish school work, chores, or duties in the workplace
- often has difficulty organizing tasks and activities
- often avoids, dislikes, or is reluctant to engage in tasks that require sustained mental effort (such as schoolwork or homework)
- often loses things necessary for tasks or activities
- is often easily distracted by extraneous stimuli
- is often forgetful in daily activities

Hyperactivity-impulsivity:

- often fidgets with hands or feet or squirms in seat
- often leaves seat in classroom or in other situations in which remaining seated is expected
- often runs about or climbs excessively in situations in which it is inappropriate (in adolescents or adults, may be limited to subjective feelings of restlessness)
- often has difficulty playing or engaging in leisure activities quietly
- is often "on the go" or often acts as if "driven by a motor"
- often talks excessively
- often blurts out answers before questions have been completed
- often has difficulty awaiting turn
- often interrupts or intrudes on others (e.g., butts into conversations or games)

It took American psychiatrists almost a century, from the time when Kraepelin first described the syndrome of manic-depression, to routinely recognize and diagnose bipolar disorders. Similarly, it took several decades for psychiatrists to routinely recognize and treat ADHD in adults. Both processes involved paradigm shifts, which do not come easily for anyone, and were not *readily* accepted by venerable psychiatric authorities and experts. I also struggled during the past decade with these shifting paradigms, in my less than venerable work as a clinical psychiatrist. I remained puzzled for the longest time in my attempts to differentiate bipolar symptoms from ADHD in my adult patients. Like most psychiatrists, I was working with the prevailing, hierarchical *DSM* paradigms for primary bipolar disorders *or* ADHD, not realizing that another paradigm shift was needed to better explain the pattern that I was beginning to observe in many of my adult patients, like Carolyn.

Chapter 4

Carolyn

Carolyn, an attractive 32-year-old office manager, called me for an appointment a few years ago at the request of her primary care doctor. He had started her on Paxil a few weeks earlier and she had been feeling worse than ever. She felt lethargic and irritable, and had been crying uncontrollably during the weekend before our meeting. She wasn't sleeping well, and was having trouble concentrating on tasks at work. She had even begun to have thoughts of suicide but, fortunately, had not acted on them. She felt embarrassed about seeing a psychiatrist, and struggled to avoid crying during our first meeting. She also seemed irritable, and was annoyed by the questions I asked her.

"I've been pulling a 'Carolyn' all weekend," she told me. When I asked her what "pulling a Carolyn" was, she told me that it was a phrase her family had used during her childhood to describe her temper tantrums and crying jags. She had always been moody, like her father, and had grown up trying to live up to her parent's demands for perfection and achievement. Schoolwork had often been difficult for her, but she had worked hard to put herself through college after her father had abandoned the family to marry his secretary. Carolyn had been successful in her career, but her personal life had been marred by a series of bad relationships with narcissistic men like her father.

She had felt very well a few years earlier after her doctor started her on the antidepressant Wellbutrin. It had dramatically improved her depression within one week of starting it, often a sign of a hidden bipolar disorder, and she had begun to take on more and more projects at work. She became vivacious and outgoing, and noticed an increased interest in dating. She also began to spend a great deal of money, on credit, to buy new clothes, and began to drink more heavily, something that is especially dangerous because Wellbutrin and alcohol withdrawal can both cause seizures. Her doctor had prescribed tranquilizers for a time to control her anxiety and insomnia then, fortunately, stopped the Wellbutrin when Carolyn continued to feel agitated.

As we reviewed the history it was clear that Carolyn had a bipolar disorder, which had been aggravated on two different occasions by antidepressants: first Wellbutrin and now Paxil. In fact, she was presenting to me in a *mixed* bipolar state on Paxil, with suicidal depression, agitation, irritability, and insomnia. This is a dangerous condition that is associated with a high incidence of attempted suicide, especially when the affected person is drinking and feeling disinhibited by alcohol. It is something that most psychiatrists have encountered frequently since the advent of SSRI antidepressants in 1988.

Carolyn, like most people in this situation, was not very happy to hear that I thought she had a bipolar disorder. Until recently, the public has had very little awareness and knowledge of bipolar spectrum disorders, and they are often thought to connote a serious, disabling mental illness, as is seen in cases of more severe bipolar disorders treated in hospitals. The denial of bipolar disorders in bipolar families is so typical that I have, at times, considered it almost a part of the "disease." Many people from bipolar families are creative, active, driven, flamboyant, and even well to do. They are resistant to the idea that such traits might be part of a "disease," or mental illness, and resent psychiatrists' attempts to

27

put them on mood stabilizers and "turn them into zombies." And who wouldn't? Many bipolar traits are useful for individuals and societies, which is why they are so prevalent in the human population. Defining the trait as a "disease" or "disorder" may be less than accurate. However, many people with bipolar spectrum disorders eventually learn to identify the ways in which their bipolar traits cause problems for themselves and others. Carolyn knew, for example, that her moodiness, impulsivity, and impaired concentration had caused problems for her throughout her life.

After we talked about treatment options, she, somewhat reluctantly, agreed to try the mood-stabilizing drug Depakote to control her mixed bipolar symptoms, and we tapered her off of the Paxil. She was not hospitalized because she was quite certain that she could call me if feeling suicidal, and also agreed to abstain from alcohol. She felt calmer and less irritable on Depakote, but became lethargic and increasingly depressed, partly, no doubt, as a result of stopping the Paxil. She agreed to stop Depakote and try lithium, which, in my experience, has often improved symptoms of bipolar depression, either alone or in combination with other mood stabilizers or antidepressants. Lithium did help somewhat, but she remained depressed, irritable, and quite anxious. We were eventually able to improve all of these symptoms with a combined regimen of lithium, Zyprexa, and the SSRI antidepressant Lexapro.

If this array of medications sounds bewildering to you, imagine how Carolyn and her husband felt! He often suggested that she toss out all of the "damn medications," which were, among other things, quite expensive, and focus on a healthier lifestyle--exercise, meditation, and a healthy diet. I certainly agreed with him about the healthier lifestyle changes, but also knew that, by themselves, they were not likely to bring her lifelong bipolar mood problems into a stable remission. That was why she had talked to her doctor about antidepressants in the first place. She also realized that she was feeling better, but remained unhappy and anxious at work. Her boss had been persistently critical of her, and was in the habit of constantly pointing out the slightest mistakes that Carolyn made in her work. It was a clear repetition of her childhood relationships with both parents. Our psychotherapy sessions focused on understanding and working through her experiences as a child of two narcissistic parents, one of whom had abandoned her at age twelve. She was able to identify the nature of her self-esteem problems and her extreme sensitivity to negative and positive feedback in her relationships.

Unfortunately, the criticism by her boss, and her despair and dread about work, continued. She came to one session in tears after she had been publicly berated for making errors on a payroll. I suspected that she was being passive-aggressive--retaliating against her critical boss-father-mother by screwing things up--or, perhaps, simply responding to negative expectations, as people often do. But, as we carefully reviewed the details of this incident, I suddenly realized that she was possibly describing symptoms of adult ADHD. I had not been routinely screening all of my adult patients for ADHD at that time, but had familiarized myself with the diagnostic criteria of adult ADHD. Carolyn and I reviewed her symptoms and found that her ADHD score was extremely high, especially on the scale of "inattentive" symptoms, which are most common, and frequently undiagnosed, in women and young girls. She described problems since childhood with daydreaming, and had great difficulty concentrating on lectures and assignments. Math was especially difficult for her, and she had always had problems focusing on "boring" columns of numbers on a ledger. Her success in her career had more to do with her work ethic and personality than with her accounting skills. In fact, she had always been forgetful of assignments and frequently lost things, like her keys, which she needed for daily tasks. All of these difficulties with concentration had existed long before we had started her on mood stabilizers, which can often aggravate ADHD symptoms.

I was nervous about prescribing stimulant medication for Carolyn, because I was quite certain that she was bipolar. She had become hypomanic twice on antidepressants, including the antidepressant Wellbutrin, which is a mild stimulant. I decided to start her on a low dose of Ritalin, a stimulant drug that had been used for many years to treat ADHD in children and, more recently, in adults. She noticed a partial improvement in her ADHD symptoms, especially as we titrated the dose carefully upwards. We then tried the more potent mixed amphetamine salt Adderall XR, and she felt dramatically better. Her dread about going to work disappeared. She felt much calmer and more confident about tackling the difficult, detail-oriented tasks at work. She also felt much less irritable, and her sleep *improved*.

I began to wonder if she truly had a bipolar disorder at all. Was this, as Drs. Edward Hallowell and John Ratey had described in their bestseller about ADHD, *Driven to Distraction,* simply a case of ADHD misdiagnosed as a bipolar disorder? But when I tried to taper Carolyn off of Zyprexa she felt extremely agitated and irritable. She couldn't sleep, and felt her mind racing. It was similar to the way she had felt earlier on Wellbutrin alone. We resumed the Zyprexa dose that had been working and she again felt well. When we later tried to reduce her lithium dose she became more depressed. The depression went away when we increased her lithium back to a therapeutic level. It seemed clear to me that the medication regimen we had ended up using was optimal and necessary for her ADHD *and* for her bipolar mood problem.

At the time that I was treating Carolyn I was still struggling with the old *DSM* tendency to hierarchically diagnose a primary condition like bipolar disorder *or* ADHD. *Either* the person had a primary bipolar disorder, which could impair their ability to concentrate on tasks, *or* they had primary ADHD, which could cause emotional reactivity. And, of course, I was not the only psychiatrist in America struggling with these issues. Even the venerable Dr. Akiskal had theorized that the childhood "hyperactivity" of his bipolar II adults had probably been an early life manifestation of a *bipolar* temperament. At the time, I had not yet discovered the research by Dr. Joseph Biederman's group at Harvard about comorbid ADHD in *children* with bipolar disorders, and I suspect-- even as I am writing this book in March of 2005--that most psychiatrists in America still have not.

Chapter 5

The Children of the Massachusetts General

For many years psychiatrists believed that childhood ADHD ended in adolescence or early adulthood. They also believed that bipolar disorders always began in adolescent and adult years. The prevailing dogma was that bipolar disorders were *very* rare, virtually non-existent, in children. But in the 1980's--and in scattered case reports dating back to the 1930's--some child psychiatrists, notably Dr. Gabrielle Carlson, began to describe what looked like bipolar disorders in children. These children presented to clinics with irritability, depression, and protracted *mixed* bipolar symptoms, rather than with the discrete manic episodes seen in many bipolar adults. In the 1990's Dr. Janet Wozniak and a group of research psychiatrists at Harvard, led by Dr. Joseph Biederman, began to publish a series of papers about children who, like Dr. Carlson's subjects, appeared to be bipolar. These children, evaluated in the Pediatric Psychopharmacology clinic of the Massachusetts General Hospital, usually presented with marked irritability and protracted mixed bipolar symptoms. They were also found to have a very high incidence of co-occurring, or "comorbid," ADHD, oppositional defiant, conduct, and anxiety disorders. In fact, *almost all of these bipolar children met full diagnostic criteria for ADHD.* Was their ADHD mainly a result of mania, or vice versa? Was it a misnomer to call them "bipolar" at all?

Subsequent research at Harvard and elsewhere, including important studies by Dr. Barbara Geller of Washington University, demonstrated that the bipolar symptoms of these children were not secondary to ADHD, or vice versa. Most of them were suffering from symptoms of both bipolar disorder *and* ADHD. What is more, the relatives of these children also seemed to exhibit a high coincidence of bipolar disorder and ADHD. In contrast, bipolar disorders originating later in life seemed to be associated with a much lower incidence of comorbid ADHD. The bipolar children seemed to comprise a distinct subpopulation of bipolar individuals who also had ADHD and anxiety disorders. Those in the psychiatric community who took notice of this research at all continued to talk about bipolar syndromes and ADHD syndromes, following the *DSM* paradigms, but not about an apparently new, integral syndrome of both disorders. In short, the familial syndrome of childhood-onset bipolar disorder with ADHD had no proper name.

Because the childhood bipolar/ADHD debate and research had occurred mainly in academic circles of child psychiatry, it also failed to impress psychiatrists focusing on adult bipolar research. In an early Systematic Treatment Enhancement Program (STEP) study, published in the *American Journal of Psychiatry in October of 2004*, there was no mention at all of ADHD in the "phenomenology" of bipolar adults being evaluated for "rapid-cycling." I was surprised when I read the article, because I had studied Dr. Biederman's data and assumed that adult academicians must have known about it. Similarly, in an earlier large-scale study of *comorbid* syndromes in bipolar adults--published in 2001in the *American Journal of Psychiatry*--there was also no mention of ADHD. As far as I could tell, no one was *looking* for ADHD in bipolar adults, despite research by Dr. Biederman's group some years earlier describing the familial syndrome of childhood-onset bipolar disorder with comorbid ADHD.

After the preliminary STEP study on rapid-cycling bipolar adults appeared in October of 2004, I did an online journal search for "bipolar" and "adult ADHD." Only a few papers had been published on this comorbid syndrome in *young* adults, mainly by child psychiatrists following cohorts of previously diagnosed children and adolescents. That, in itself, was understandable, because child psychiatrists had only recently begun to diagnose bipolar disorders in children. Two notable exceptions were papers published by Dr. Gary Sachs and by Dr. Biederman's group, both from the Massachusetts General Hospital. In the first of these, published in the *American Journal of Psychiatry* in 2000, Dr. Sachs and his colleagues found that bipolar adults with ADHD had a history of *early-onset* bipolar symptoms, typically prior to age 19. In the second, published in the November 2003 issue of the *Journal of Child and Adolescent Psychopharmacology*, Dr. Biederman and his colleagues compared three cohorts of bipolar adults who had experienced the onset of bipolar symptoms in either childhood, adolescence, or adulthood. It confirmed a high incidence of ADHD in the early-onset bipolar adults (63%), and also found that the early-onset bipolar adults had a very high incidence of comorbid *anxiety disorders*, with 75% meeting diagnostic criteria for two or more anxiety disorders. The only other study I could find on the subject was a paper published in the *Journal of Affective Disorders* in 2000 by Dr. Franck Schurhoff and his colleagues at the Salpetriere Hospital in Paris. It showed that *hospitalized* adults with *early-onset* bipolar disorders had a very high incidence of *panic disorder* (21%), *mixed* bipolar (30%), and *psychotic* symptoms (47%) compared to hospitalized adults with later-onset bipolar disorders. But Dr. Schurhoff, like most of the adult researchers, did not mention ADHD in his study of bipolar adults.

As I reviewed the numbers, I realized that Dr. Biederman's 2003 study had identified only *twenty* adults with the syndrome of early-onset bipolar disorder and ADHD, which is called in experimental medicine an "n" of 20 with the letter "n" indicating the number of subjects. It occurred to me that, over the years, I had probably treated hundreds of adults, often with less than optimal results, who had experienced *early-onset* bipolar mood problems with comorbid anxiety disorders. Many were still in treatment with me, and had often been taking multiple medications to control their mood and anxiety problems. Were they, possibly, undiagnosed examples of Biederman's syndrome of *early-onset bipolar disorder with ADHD and anxiety*? Was Carolyn? And, if so, could they be more effectively treated with stimulants, as Carolyn had been?

I also noticed that Dr. Biederman's study showed that, although the early-onset bipolar adults had a "lower socio-economic status" than the later-onset subjects, the early-onset group had higher IQ's, *despite suffering from ADHD,* a condition that would likely impair their performance on IQ tests. Was it possible, I wondered, that millions of adults with early-onset bipolar disorders were struggling in life because *psychiatrists had not been diagnosing or treating their inherited, comorbid ADHD?* Then, as I was brushing my teeth one evening before going to bed, brooding about these questions, it occurred to me that one answer might be staring back at me from the bathroom mirror. My young daughters were, apparently, *both* bipolar and my wife was not. Their childhood-onset bipolar gene(s) must have come from me. I had found an adult "n" of at least one.

Chapter 6

Physician, Heal Thyself

Doctors are notoriously bad patients, and I was no exception. Many doctors, myself included, have narcissistic personality traits and are reluctant to admit that they are defective. Many are also "counter-dependent" and have difficulty asking for help. Although I had undergone four years of psychoanalytic therapy as part of my training, which was immensely helpful, I had never undergone a modern, "descriptive" psychiatric evaluation. And, despite being a psychiatrist, I had never succeeded in accurately diagnosing myself. For one thing, there were aspects of my history that did not fit clearly into the well-defined categories of the various *Diagnostic and Statistical Manuals* used by American psychiatrists in the late twentieth century. It did not occur to me until the fall of 2004 that I might have an inherited psychiatric syndrome, not clearly *named* by the *Diagnostic and Statistical Manual,* which could explain the constellation of symptoms in my own history.

I knew that I had been a moody child, and I distinctly remember feeling *very* depressed at age twelve after a friend died of leukemia and two close friends had moved out of state. I also had frequent temper tantrums during my childhood, and was nicknamed the "belligerent baboon" by my oldest sister, who was, herself, no paragon of equanimity. I never slept well as a child, and could recall lying awake for hours at night without feeling tired the next day. I learned to read during the summer before first grade and read book after book all summer in rapid succession, often lying awake in bed with a flashlight. During the second week of my first grade year I told my teacher that I had finished reading the textbook for the year--a thick blue tome entitled *We Are Neighbors*-- and that I wanted to read something else. She didn't believe me, and ordered me to sit by her desk in a "dunce's" chair. When I protested, she opened the textbook and started to quiz me in front of the class. She turned to a story toward the end of the book, called *Papa Was A Riot*, and told me to tell her about it. When I did so, she smiled and looked surprised. I was moved the following week to a different class and placed in a reading group called the "Lions" with four other children.

I continued to experience episodes of depression in my teens, including some weeks in college when I slept heavily and had great difficulty getting out of bed for classes. At other times, I would stay up most of the night solving calculus and physics problems, reading books, and writing papers about philosophy and history. During one such hypomanic period I decided to run for the student government and went door to door through the dormitories introducing myself to people. More often, I was reclusive and sullen. At such times I immersed myself in the gloomy existentialist writings of Sartre and Camus, concluding that life was, indeed, absurd. During my first year of medical school at Harvard I became so lethargic and withdrawn that my friends at Vanderbilt Hall, the student dormitory, called me a "worm," and joked that I needed shock treatments, which was not far wrong. I could barely drag myself to classes, and even dropped out of school briefly until a sympathetic dean convinced me to stay the course.

Finally, at age 33, after many trials and tribulations, I discovered that I had a disorder of the endocrine system, hypothyroidism, which is known to cause depression and lethargy. I took thyroid hormone pills and felt better after several weeks, but was still depressed. I decided to try Prozac, but felt persistently sluggish and miserable for six long weeks. Then I tried a medication that worked surprisingly well. I began to feel less depressed and less irritable. I slept better and woke up feeling awake and alert. The medication was desipramine, a tricyclic antidepressant that had been used since the 1960's to treat depression. It was known for its ability to block the synaptic reuptake of norepinephrine, unlike the modern selective serotonin reuptake inhibitors (SSRI's) like Prozac, which worked by blocking the reuptake of serotonin.

I had long known about the norepinephrine/serotonin issue in clinical depression because as a medical student at Harvard I had taken a tutorial course with Dr. Joseph Schildkraut. He is known in psychiatric history for his publication of a paper in 1965 about the "catecholamine hypothesis" of clinical depression. It was a somewhat controversial hypothesis at the time, which proposed that symptoms of clinical depression were caused by abnormal brain activity of catecholamine neurotransmitters. "Interpretive," psychoanalytic psychiatry was then in its heyday, and the catecholamine hypothesis called for a paradigm shift that few were open to making. In his paper, Dr. Schildkraut summarized the pharmacological data supporting his hypothesis, and he spent many subsequent years at Harvard trying, unsuccessfully, to find a practical assay of catecholamine metabolites that could serve as a guide to the classification and treatment of depressive disorders.

The prevailing practice in the pre-Prozac era was to treat depression with partially serotonergic drugs like the tricyclic antidepressants amitriptyline (Elavil) or nortriptyline (Pamelor), and to switch to the more selectively noradrenergic drug desipramine if patients had a poor response to the serotonergic drugs. Prozac--and the other

SSRI's: Zoloft, Paxil, Luvox, Celexa, and Lexapro--achieved great popularity after 1988, and the older tricyclic drugs, including desipramine, fell into disuse.   The tricyclics caused side effects that were not problematic with the SSRI's, and were also much more toxic in overdoses.   New antidepressants also appeared in the post-Prozac era that increased norepinephrine activity--Wellbutrin, Effexor, and, recently, Cymbalta--so physicians found little reason to use desipramine.

Nevertheless, in the winter of 1990, desipramine worked well for me. My wife noticed that I seemed much less irritable and ceased driving like a Bostonian. I felt more patient and organized in my work, and continued taking desipramine for the next twelve months. Whenever I tried to taper off of it in subsequent years, my wife and I noticed that I became much more irritable and negative about everything, which I attributed to a resurgence of dysthymia, or chronic depression. In all, I continued to take desipramine for ten years, and they were good years. I enjoyed my work, bought a house in a neighborhood I loved, became a father, took up gardening, and read voraciously in my free time. But I also noticed that my old bursts of creative energy disappeared with the irritability. My musical instruments--guitars, violin, mandolin, piano, and drums--had been gathering dust for almost a decade. I was calm, almost to a fault, or--as one of my colleagues said to me one day on a hectic hospital ward--"unflappable." I had, in a sense, ceased flapping my wings, ceased flying.

Then, in the spring of 2000, when my oldest daughter was finishing kindergarten, I decided to have LASIK eye surgery. I was severely near-sighted and had been wearing contact lenses for over twenty years. I always disliked wearing glasses, partly out of vanity, but also because I could never ski or play tennis without getting sweat and fog all over the lenses. However, before having the measurements for the LASIK, I had to stop taking desipramine because it altered my vision through its effect on the lens muscles of my eyes. I stopped the desipramine and had the LASIK surgery in April.

Afterwards, to my relief, things looked swell. They didn't exactly look *great*: my left eye was so severely astigmatic and myopic that it could not be fully corrected by surgery. Nor did I have the whole world on a plate, but I do recall feeling good as the summer approached: working in the garden and spending as much time as possible out of doors. I also began to think about playing my guitars and other musical instruments that had been gathering dust for years. I couldn't remember the last time I had wanted to pick them up, other than a brief gig at our hospital Christmas party with some colleagues. Had it been ten years? I saw an advertisement from a local music store that June and noticed that they were selling a multi-track digital recording deck that even a psychiatrist could afford. I decided, somewhat impulsively, to buy it, and I set up a recording "studio" in my basement. My wife was a bit surprised, and wondered if I was having a sort of low budget, mid-life crisis.

The Fourth of July weekend was approaching when I found a fake book of Beatles songs at the local music store. I stayed up late one night playing around with the bass and electric guitars, and started to burn some tracks using the new digital recorder. I had to transpose the Lennon-McCartney tenor lines half an octave down, but the book and the recorder were surprisingly easy to use. I could almost hear the old Beatles records playing in my head, note-for-note. The next day I begged off of the planned holiday weekend trek to the mountains to visit my in-laws. I relished the idea of having a weekend of studio silence, which was rare in a household with two young children. My daughters had mainly wanted to play with their cousins, in any case, and my wife wanted to spend time with her family.

That weekend was something of a blur. I became so absorbed in recording guitar, bass, and vocal tracks that I stopped for only a few minutes here and there to run upstairs for a sandwich or a coke. I remember being truly surprised to discover that it was getting dark outside one evening on a day when I had been recording tracks in the basement studio since dawn. I also remember falling asleep on the floor after midnight one night, only to wake up a few hours later to record more tracks. By the time my wife and children returned home, on Sunday night, I was completing the vocal tracks on the last two songs in the anthology. I heard doors slamming and footsteps through my headphones and realized that the weekend jam session was over. I had recorded over twenty-five songs in multiple parts, and my first digital album, "It's Such a Feeling," was finished. My fingers were raw and bruised and my back and shoulders ached.

During the next two years I spent several such weekends "jamming" with my one man studio "band" in the basement, recording multiple albums, fourteen in all, in a variety of genres: 1960's soul, acoustic blues, reggae, jazz, folk rock, Celtic folk, and even Gregorian and Russian chants. I was puzzled by this behavior, attributing it in part to my acquisition of new recording technology. I certainly wondered if I might be *hypomanic*: goal-directed, creative, and energetic, at least for one or two days. But, if I were hypomanic, why was it happening only after I had *stopped* taking an antidepressant that I had taken for almost ten years? Why had I never experienced bursts of creative energy, or other symptoms of hypomania, during a ten-year period on desipramine? Most people with bipolar tendencies are likely to experience hypomania, if at all, when taking an antidepressant. It was this *calming* effect of desipramine, more than anything, which led me to doubt that I was bipolar, even when it became painfully obvious during the next two years that both of my daughters were suffering from bipolar disorders.

I knew that desipramine, in addition to its antidepressant effects, had been shown by Dr. Biederman's group at Harvard to improve ADHD symptoms in children and adults, and I began to wonder if I had some type of adult ADHD. It seemed unlikely to me at the time because, if anything, I had always had an unusual ability to concentrate on things that interested me. I had aced almost every test I had ever taken in my life. I still remember the day that a very strict Spanish teacher at my old high school--a woman who used to help write the Spanish Advanced Placement exams in America--announced to our class that a student had "maxed out" one of her exams, receiving a perfect score, for the first time in over ten years. That test involved fairly strict attention to complex details of verb conjugations and grammar. Similarly, in college at Brown, I had aced critical examinations in multiple subjects, including the grueling general and organic chemistry exams taken by hundreds of competitive pre-medical students. On those tests I had received comments from professors like: "A+ with high distinction. Your score was significantly higher than the entire class," and, "Congratulations, your score was the highest of all!" A physics professor had recruited me to tutor students for his class, and the chemistry faculty had even awarded me a special scholarship from Eastman Kodak, mainly based on some test scores.

So, if there was one thing that I could do well, it was to concentrate on details that interested me. I couldn't imagine that I had ADHD. It *was* true that I was easily bored throughout my life. My mind wandered readily, and I had a lifelong habit of doodling and daydreaming. I fell asleep during lectures that I found dull, especially in medical school, and could hardly stay awake in my third year of medical school during the endless hallway discourses by physicians of internal medicine. I joked about "holding up the walls" on medical rounds at the Massachusetts General Hospital but, in truth, it was no laughing matter. My inability to concentrate on necessary medical tasks seemed to me, and probably to others, a defect of character. One physician said that I "lacked discipline," which seemed puzzling to me, because I had always been a hard worker. During tasks that interested me--interviews with psychiatric patients or surgical procedures in an operating room--I could become so absorbed in what was happening that I lost track of time: a trait of many people with ADHD, called "hyperfocusing." But I had great difficulty sustaining attention on the necessary, mundane details of medical work. My cognitive style was to quickly arrive at a diagnosis, to bring essential details together in a kind of gestalt, or synthesis: to go to the heart of the matter. I could solve a challenging diagnostic conundrum--as I did for our medical student's report at the Massachusetts General Hospital grand rounds conference, published in the *New England Journal of Medicine*--but fall asleep over a list of medical symptoms that had been split into groups for methodical "rule outs." Although I had, typically, done very well on my Medical Board examinations, I knew that I was not meant to be a doctor of internal medicine, or any sort of doctor who needed to concentrate carefully on details that I did not find stimulating. I had nearly fallen asleep during a one-day attempt at an anesthesiology clerkship in medical school and had promptly switched to a different elective.

Another problem that I began to notice in medical school was anxiety. I had been somewhat nervous about public speaking since

43

childhood, but had my first episode of *panic* while presenting a case to a team of surgeons at the Massachusetts General in my third year of medical school. As I began to speak, I suddenly felt my heart racing, and became so flooded with panic that I could hardly think, much less talk. It was one of the most humiliating moments of my life. A friendly surgical resident tactfully presented the case, and later told me that my attacks of "performance" anxiety could probably be controlled by a new drug called propranolol, used to treat high blood pressure. Propranolol works by blocking Beta-adrenergic receptors, and was the first of the so-called "Beta-blockers" on the market. In addition to being used in the treatment of high blood pressure and migraines, it had been found to block many of the physical symptoms of performance anxiety, or "stage fright," without causing mental confusion or addiction, as the widely used benzodiazepine tranquilizers were known to do. The resident gave me a prescription for propranolol, and it worked so well that I continued to use it for many years in situations where I had to speak in public. Twenty years later I realized that my anxiety symptoms were probably part of the same psychiatric syndrome of early-onset bipolar disorder that I finally identified in my daughters, in myself, and in many of my adult patients.

I wish that I could say that I had readily identified this syndrome in 2000 after stopping desipramine. In retrospect, all of the data were sitting there, especially the studies from Dr. Biederman's group showing that almost all children with bipolar disorder had ADHD, and that there is a familial aspect to this syndrome. Unfortunately, it didn't happen that way, perhaps partly because I was not yet aware that my *daughters* were bipolar, and I had not studied the child psychiatric literature. In my defense I can only say that no one *else* in adult psychiatry seemed to see the pattern either, or, if they had, they had not published anything about it. In any case, I was finally able to accurately diagnose myself in the fall of 2004. I had a bipolar type II disorder, with onset in childhood. I also found, to my surprise, that I scored very highly on an ADHD symptom checklist adapted for adults. In addition, I had an anxiety disorder with characteristics of social anxiety, atypical panic (in that my panic symptoms were triggered by specific stimuli, rather than being "spontaneous" as in true panic disorder), and generalized anxiety disorders. Since my diagnosis had no proper name in the adult psychiatric nomenclature, I decided to call it the *Childhood-Onset Bipolar Attention Deficit*, or "COBAD," syndrome.

I sought treatment with a psychiatric colleague who was open to hearing about my diagnostic notions, and had a very good response to a medication regimen that was working well for some of my adult patients with similar symptoms. It consisted in taking the stimulant drug Adderall XR in the morning, and a low dose of the mood stabilizer Zyprexa at bedtime. On this regimen I felt better than I had ever felt in my life, though, like Julie and Carolyn, I did not feel *hypomanic*. I felt more like Rip Van Winkle. As I calmly looked back on the previous forty years of my life, I realized that I had been "out of it" much of the time. I had certainly worked hard, but had been moody and driven, usually without thinking carefully about where I was driving. The academic and creative work that I had accomplished had usually been done in brief, frenetic bursts--like my musical recordings--rather than in patient, thoughtful steps. If I lost interest in a project, ceased to find it stimulating, as I often did, I left it unfinished. Like Faust, I had read stacks and stacks of books on various subjects--astrophysics, Byzantine history, evolutionary theory, Russian literature, and theology--only to abandon my intentions of writing a book when I lost interest in the project. (If Doctor Faustus didn't suffer from

45

the COBAD syndrome, the dramatist Christopher Marlowe certainly must have.) I could quickly plan and do the intense spade work for a garden project, but often relied upon my wife to carefully complete the necessary details that brought it to fruition. Or, as author Thom Hartman has described in his book *The Edison Gene*, my cognitive and emotional traits were, perhaps, adaptive for the life of the hunter-gatherers who had been my distant--and perhaps not so distant*--ancestors, but had certainly not been very conducive to optimal functioning in the post-Neolithic society around me.

*My father's mother always insisted that her father--the son of an itinerant prospector--had been the first Anglo child born in Colorado Indian Territory.

Chapter 7

You See What You Look For

A surgical resident that I knew during my third year at Harvard Medical School used to say: "You see what you look for, and you look for what you know." In my twenty years of work as a psychiatrist I had learned to look for bipolar disorders in depressed patients. I had, more recently, begun to actively look for *ADHD* in my adult patients, and was surprised that so many of them had ADHD, including many, like myself, who had done well in school. Some were even accountants and successful professional people in fields requiring intense mental concentration. I came to realize that many of these adults with ADHD could concentrate extremely well, or *hyperfocus*, when they felt challenged or stimulated by fear or genuine enthusiasm. In neurochemical terms, they could hyperfocus when their "adrenaline" levels (norepinephrine and dopamine) were naturally elevated. When bored, they had difficulty sustaining attention and focus, and their work and personal lives suffered. By increasing their norepinephrine and dopamine activity with stimulants, they could sustain concentration and focus on important tasks that they otherwise found dull.

Once I had finally recognized the existence of the COBAD syndrome--childhood-onset bipolar disorder with ADHD and anxiety--I began to look for it, systematically, in my adult patients. I had been treating a large number of adults with bipolar disorders for many years. Most of them had bipolar type II disorders, with chronic, mixed depression and hypomanic irritability. I had not recently been treating many people with more severe bipolar type I disorders--those who had experienced full manic episodes--because our University Hospital had closed its private ward five years earlier, and I had moved at that time to a private office off campus with several colleagues. It had become difficult for me to safely coordinate transitions between inpatient and outpatient care for seriously ill patients. A growing cadre of "hospitalists"-- psychiatrists who only treated patients in the hospital--was providing the inpatient psychiatric care in our community. I found that they rarely called me to review the medication histories of my patients, or to discuss discharge plans, and, under these circumstances, I became less and less willing to undertake the care of people who might require hospitalization as part of their treatment. (The underfunded, shrinking psychiatric infrastructure of America is, perhaps, a subject for an entirely different book.)

In any case, as I began to look for the COBAD syndrome in my adult outpatients, I found that it was *everywhere*. Time and time again I found significant lifelong ADHD in my adult bipolar patients. As I reviewed their histories, I noticed that most of them had experienced significant mood problems in childhood years, though few had been diagnosed or treated in childhood. Most of them also described lifelong problems with generalized anxiety, panic attacks, and/or social phobia. Like me, most of them had also experienced fluctuating sleep cycles throughout their lives, along with an array of ADHD symptoms. Many women with the syndrome had characteristically high scores on the "inattentive" ADHD subscale. They often described family members who had similar symptoms, and a high incidence of familial alcoholism, violence, and post-traumatic stress disorder (PTSD) caused by traumatic family experiences.

Many of my newly diagnosed COBAD syndrome adult patients had been treated, often for years, with combinations of mood stabilizers and antidepressants that had achieved less than optimal results. The research literature has documented very well the often chronic, unsatisfactory course of treatment for many such bipolar adults. I began to realize that these less than optimal outcomes were often a result of *chronically undiagnosed, untreated ADHD*. Adult psychiatrists, and many child psychiatrists, have simply not been aware of the existence of the COBAD syndrome in bipolar patients. In addition, psychiatrists who *do* diagnose and treat ADHD routinely have often been reluctant to prescribe stimulants for people with bipolar disorders. Stimulants can aggravate bipolar disorders, causing manic and even psychotic symptoms such as hallucinations and delusions. In fact, they can cause such symptoms even in people who are *not* bipolar, as seen in people who are abusing amphetamines or cocaine.

The approach that I began to use in treating my COBAD syndrome adult patients, as in Carolyn's case, was adapted from standard psychiatric procedures for the treatment of bipolar disorders, adult ADHD, and anxiety disorders. It involved first stabilizing moods with reliable and effective mood stabilizers, then adding doses of stimulant medication *if and when there were no signs or symptoms of hypomania*. I would titrate the stimulant dosage--usually Ritalin LA or the long acting mixed amphetamine salt Adderall XR--to a dosage that reduced ADHD symptoms to a minimum. If noticing symptoms of hypomania or psychosis, I would then adjust the medication dosages to control the emerging symptoms.

Roger, for example, was a 52-year-old public relations executive who came to see me, at the request of his primary care doctor, shortly after I had clarified my thinking about the COBAD syndrome in the fall of 2004. He had always been fairly energetic and outgoing before becoming depressed a few months earlier. His doctor had started him on the antidepressant Wellbutrin, and it had improved his depression for several weeks before it "stopped working." His doctor had then started him on the SSRI antidepressant Lexapro. Shortly after starting Lexapro Roger began to feel agitated and irritable, and had trouble sleeping. He stopped the Lexapro one month before seeing me, but continued to feel depressed, irritable, and anxious. He was sleeping only three or four hours per night, despite taking a "double" dose of the sedative Ambien. When I saw Roger in my office he appeared quite moody and distracted, and had difficulty concentrating on our conversation.

It seemed clear that Roger, like Carolyn, had a bipolar disorder, and was experiencing mixed symptoms of depression and hypomania that had been exacerbated by antidepressants. He and his wife confirmed that he had been energetic, outgoing, and irritable since at least high school years. He also scored highly on an ADHD symptom checklist. He had, apparently, never been severely or *persistently* depressed until he was in his forties. His father, an alcoholic, had been diagnosed with a bipolar disorder and had taken lithium for many years, but had "never done very well" on any of the medications he had taken. We discussed my impression that Roger had a type of bipolar disorder with ADHD, and began a trial of the mood stabilizer Depakote, which is often helpful in the treatment of mixed bipolar states.

During the next week Roger felt calmer, but he complained of feeling more depressed and lethargic. He was having difficulty functioning at work, but refused to take time off for fear of losing his job. He agreed to a trial of lithium, and felt less depressed during the next two weeks as we simultaneously tapered him off of Depakote. However, he called me one week later, during an out of town business trip, complaining of insomnia and anxiety. He did not want to resume Depakote, so I called a prescription of the mood-stabilizing drug Zyprexa to a pharmacy in the city where he was staying. When I saw him a week later he was feeling *much* better on lithium and low dose Zyprexa, but complained of persistent difficulty concentrating on projects at work and at home. He was not exhibiting symptoms of hypomania, and had a persistently elevated ADHD score. We, therefore, started Adderall XR and he began to feel much better, without emergent hypomania. He felt more organized, and his wife told me that he was much less irritable. On lithium, low dose Zyprexa, and Adderall XR his mood remained positive, and his concentration and work performance were greatly improved.

Chapter 8

"The Best I Have Ever Felt in My Life"

Roger's case, like Carolyn's, was typical of many that followed. Most of my COBAD syndrome adult patients had been treated, often for years, according to established standards of care for adults with bipolar disorders. They had usually been taking mood stabilizers, either alone or in combination with antidepressants, and had been struggling to survive and cope with the demands of daily living. Practicing psychiatrists were often criticized by "experts "in the 1990's for prescribing antidepressants for such depressed bipolar adults. I had done so at times in a desperate attempt to keep my patients from committing suicide. (Later studies eventually showed what practitioners had known for years: that many people with bipolar depression clearly benefited from adjunctive antidepressants.) Now, as I began to identify and treat the highly prevalent *ADHD* symptoms of my bipolar patients with stimulants, I was concerned that I might worsen their mood disorders, and also be condemned by the "experts" who used to condemn antidepressant use.

Instead, something remarkable happened. Then it happened again and again, day after day. As I had seen with Carolyn, my patients would come into my office and say: "This is the best I have ever felt in my life." On screening for hypomania, most of them described feeling less agitated and far less irritable on stimulants. They often noticed improved sleep, without hypomanic symptoms such as racing thoughts, pressured speech, or impulsivity. It was the same scene that I had witnessed earlier with the

ECT patient Dr. Dodson had sent to me on Adderall and Zoloft. Not only were their ADHD symptoms disappearing, often for the first time in their lives, but their moods were also improving. They were sleeping more soundly, and one even noticed that her psychotic symptoms, the "weird feelings" that someone was standing behind her, had disappeared. (These "weird feelings" had been the subject of considerable psychodynamic work, focusing on trauma, prior to treating her ADHD with Adderall.) Some of my patients *did* experience hypomanic symptoms on stimulants, and needed to stop them to maintain mood stability. But those cases were the exception to the rule, and often occurred in people who had been intolerant of mood stabilizers, or had stopped taking them without telling me. In all, about 80% of my adult bipolar II outpatients with the COBAD syndrome were able to achieve a stable remission of their ADHD symptoms on mood stabilizers and stimulants without becoming hypomanic.

In this regard, I cannot emphasize enough the importance of using stimulant medications *carefully* in the treatment of any ADHD syndrome. This is a concern of mine with the recent widespread advertising of medications, especially Straterra, for the treatment of ADHD. If, as Dr. Biederman's data indicates, 20-25% of *children* with ADHD also have bipolar disorders, there is a significant public health risk with widespread indiscriminate use of Straterra and stimulants in *adults* with ADHD who have undiagnosed bipolar disorders. The end result could be similar to the epidemic of hypomania seen in bipolar adults treated with SSRI's in the 1990's, and even to this day.

The good news is that millions of people with the COBAD syndrome are likely to benefit greatly from the proper diagnosis and treatment of their condition with mood stabilizers and stimulant medications. My own experience is that they will notice a dramatic improvement in symptoms that have caused problems for them throughout their lives. This is especially encouraging for many adults diagnosed with bipolar disorders who have had persistent, inadequate treatment responses to "standard" psychiatric treatment. Our current mood stabilizers and "atypical antipsychotics" are clearly helpful in preventing *manic* symptoms, but less useful for the chronic depression that has been the main long-term problem for so many people with bipolar disorders. In addition, the mood stabilizers do not, by themselves, resolve the *ADHD* symptoms. In fact, mood stabilizers may *worsen* ADHD symptoms in people with the COBAD syndrome by interfering with catecholamine neurotransmission. The optimal approach, in my opinion, is to find a combination of mood stabilizers and stimulant medications that treat both the bipolar symptoms and the ADHD symptoms without aggravating either.

While a medication regimen may work well for one person and not another, I have developed an empirical approach that has worked well for most of the COBAD syndrome adults in my practice. It is consistent with the limited published data on *children* treated for bipolar disorders and ADHD, including the single controlled study that was published in the January 2005 issue of the *American Journal of Psychiatry*. That study appeared after I had written a summary of my ideas about the COBAD syndrome and its treatment for a conference with the psychiatrist treating my daughters. By that time, I was convinced that my daughters were suffering from untreated ADHD as part of the COBAD syndrome, and that they could benefit from the approach that was working for me, and for many of my adult COBAD syndrome patients. Since then, I have become even more convinced that the proper diagnosis and treatment of the COBAD syndrome will substantially improve the prognosis of millions of people currently diagnosed and treated as merely bipolar. It is this conviction that, ultimately, led me to write this book, and to present my findings in the following letter to Dr. Nancy Andreasen, the editor-in-chief of the *American Journal of Psychiatry*, in March of 2005.

THE DIAGNOSIS AND TREATMENT OF CHILDHOOD-ONSET BIPOLAR ADHD (COBAD) SYNDROME IN AN ADULT OUTPATIENT SAMPLE

During the past decade research in child psychiatry has identified a familial syndrome of childhood-onset bipolar disorder *and* ADHD, characteristic of almost all children with bipolar disorder.[1-2] In this population, the ADHD has been shown to be an essential aspect of the disorder, not a mere epiphenomenon of mania or of the mixed bipolar states experienced by these children and their first-degree relatives.[3] Because it has no proper name, I will refer to this psychiatric syndrome here as the COBAD syndrome, an acronym for Childhood-Onset Bipolar Attention-Deficit syndrome. The COBAD syndrome has been estimated to account for 20-25% of all childhood ADHD, indicating a syndrome with possible high prevalence in the adult population.[4] Yet surprisingly little published research has appeared describing the COBAD syndrome in adults. Akiskal's 1995 prospective study of depressed adults showed that those with a constellation of symptoms suggestive of ADHD, and early-onset mood problems, had a prospective course of bipolar II disorder.[5]

Along these lines, I recently identified 27 adult outpatients seen during a one-year period in my practice who met *DSM-IV* criteria for Bipolar II Disorder *with onset of mood problems in childhood years, and comorbid ADHD*. A diagnostic assessment of ADHD symptoms was made only when the patients were not exhibiting signs or symptoms of hypomania. The patients were initially treated with a mood-stabilizing regimen, usually including lithium, and were then started on stimulant medication when they were not exhibiting any residual signs or symptoms of hypomania. The dosage of stimulant medication, usually Adderall XR or Ritalin LA, was titrated to control their ADHD symptoms.

The results have been remarkable. The vast majority of these COBAD syndrome adult patients (22/27 or 81%) experienced a marked reduction in their ADHD symptoms *and* a general improvement in mood stability, with reduced irritability, anxiety, and insomnia. I have seen a very low incidence of hypomania, cycling, or psychosis during a follow up period ranging from two to twelve months. Three of the five who developed mood instability on stimulants had a history of questionable compliance with medications. Controlled research is called for, but I suspect, and hope, that the well-known poor prognosis of many bipolar II patients, especially those with early-onset symptoms, will improve dramatically with increased recognition and treatment of what appears to be a prevalent COBAD syndrome in adults.

1. Biederman, J, Faraone, S, Mick, E, Wozniak, J, Chen, L, Quellette, C, Marrs, A, Moore, P, Garcia, J, Mennin, D & Lelon, E. (1996). Attention-deficit hyperactivity disorder and juvenile mania: an overlooked comorbidity? *J Am Acad Child Adolescent Psychiatry*, 35, 997-1008.
2. Faraone, S, Biederman, J, Mennin, D, Wozniak, J & Spencer, C. (1997). Attention-deficit hyperactivity disorder with bipolar disorder: a familial subtype? *J Am Acad Child Adolesc Psychiatry*, 36, 1378-1387.
3. Milberger, S, Biederman, J, Faraone, S, Murphy, J & Tsuang, M. (1995). Attention-deficit hyperactivity disorder and comorbid disorders: issues of overlapping symptoms. *Am J Psychiatry*, 152, 1793-1799.
4. Biederman, J, Faraone, S, Milberger, S, Guite, J, Mick, E, Chen, L, Mennin, D, Marrs, A, Ouellette, C, Moore, P, Spencer, T, Norman, D, Wilens, T, Kraus, I & Perrin, J. (1996). A prospective 4-year follow-up study of attention-deficit hyperactivity and related disorders. *Arch Gen Psych*, 53, 437-446.
5. Akiskal, H, Maser, J, Zeller, P, Endicott, J, Coryell, W, Keller, M, Warshaw, M, Clayton, P & Goodwin, F. (1995). Switching from unipolar to bipolar II: an 11-year prospective study of clinical and temperamental predictors in 559 patients. *Arch Gen Psychiatry*, 52, 114-123.

Chapter 9

COBAD Syndrome I: Diagnosis

The essential diagnostic criteria of the COBAD syndrome are a history of ADHD *and* bipolar disorder originating in childhood years. Hypomanic symptoms may often be unrecognized and unreported, but most people with bipolar disorders have experienced depression. In practical terms, *any person diagnosed with depression should be carefully screened for a history of hypomania and ADHD, and anyone diagnosed with ADHD should be carefully screened for any history of hypomania or depression.* As Dr. Akiskal and others have shown, depression beginning before the age of twenty is *often* an early manifestation of a bipolar disorder. Since 50-90% of adolescent- and child-onset bipolar disorders, respectively, co-occur with ADHD, it is likely that *many people who experienced significant mood problems prior to age 19 may have an undiagnosed COBAD syndrome.* Conversely, based upon the published data, 20-25% of children with ADHD, perhaps 1-2% of all children, and many of their first-degree relatives, have the COBAD syndrome. Extrapolating from the available data, the COBAD syndrome is probably highly prevalent in the human population, *especially in milder forms that are not likely to present to research-oriented psychiatric clinics* like those of the Massachusetts General Hospital.

In supporting a diagnosis of the COBAD syndrome, there should be a recognizable family history of the syndrome in first-degree relatives, though it may be expressed in variable degrees of severity in different members of a family, as with many genetically determined conditions.

The pattern of bipolarity seen in the COBAD syndrome, both in the research literature--e.g., Dr. Akiskal's 1995 study--and in my own personal and professional experience, is often that of bipolar II disorder with chronic, rapid-cycling and mixed states. Irritability and depression are prominent, often throughout the life cycle, as are anxiety disorders and substance abuse. Whether the symptoms are severe enough to be diagnosed and treated as mental *disorders* in a given case is a matter of clinical judgment and experience, as is the case in the treatment of bipolar spectrum disorders generally.

A logical approach to diagnosing the COBAD syndrome is to first clarify whether a person has ever experienced symptoms of mania or hypomania. Hypomania is the sine qua non of bipolar disorder, but its history may be hidden. I have sometimes failed, initially, to detect a prior history of hypomania in COBAD syndrome patients that I have treated (e.g., the case of Sandra in Chapter 11). The full *DSM-IV* criteria for hypomania are listed in Chapter 2, but may be summarized as *a distinct period of a persistently elevated, expansive, or irritable mood lasting for several days, accompanied by symptoms such as inflated self-esteem, a decreased need for sleep, racing thoughts, talkativeness, and increased involvement in goal-directed or pleasurable activities.* A practical screening test for hypomania-- used in research on bipolar mood disorders--is the *Mood Disorder Questionnaire*, or MDQ, shown below. A score of *seven* or more positives on this scale has been shown to have 90% specificity in detecting bipolar hypomania with 73% sensitivity.

Mood Disorder Questionnaire

1. Has there ever been a period of time when you were not your usual self and...

...you felt so good or so hyper that other people thought you were not your normal self, or you were so hyper that you got into trouble?	Yes	No
...you were so irritable that you shouted at people or started fights or arguments?	Yes	No
...you felt much more self-confident than usual?	Yes	No
...you got much less sleep than usual and found you didn't really miss it?	Yes	No
...you were much more talkative or spoke faster than usual?	Yes	No
...thoughts raced through your head or you couldn't slow your mind down?	Yes	No
...you were so easily distracted by things around you that you had trouble concentrating or staying on track?	Yes	No
...you had much more energy than usual?	Yes	No
...you were much more active or did many more things than usual?	Yes	No
you were much more social or outgoing than usual; for example, you telephoned friends in the middle of the night?	Yes	No
...you were much more interested in sex than usual?	Yes	No
...you did things that were unusual for you or that other people might have thought were excessive, foolish, or risky?	Yes	No
...spending money got you or your family into trouble?	Yes	No

2. If you checked YES to more than one of the above, have several of these ever happened during the *same period* of *time?*

       YES   NO

3. How much of a problem did any of these cause you - like being unable to work; having family, money, or legal troubles; getting into arguments or fights?

   No Problem   Minor Problem   Moderate Problem   Serious Problem

In addition to a history of mania or hypomania, a person with the COBAD syndrome must meet diagnostic criteria for ADHD. This diagnosis can be made with reasonable reliability by reviewing a history of ADHD symptoms beginning in childhood and persisting throughout life. Studies have confirmed the reliability of self-report scales for adult ADHD and, if anything, many adults with ADHD tend to *under* report their ADHD symptoms. Collateral history from a family member can usually help to confirm the diagnosis. It is important to note that some symptoms of ADHD can be caused by other mental disorders, especially hypomania. However, if the symptoms are a result of hypomania they typically have a more episodic course, occurring only during periods of elevated mood (either irritability or elation) along with other symptoms of hypomania.

ADHD experts have developed a variety of rating scales to diagnose the disorder in children and adults, and there is continued debate and discussion in the psychiatric community about which scales may be most valid and useful. Dr. Paul Wender, an early pioneer in the diagnosis and treatment of ADHD in children and adults, developed the Utah rating scale. Another scale that has been used for many years to assess ADHD is the Connors scale. Both scales have been adapted for diagnosis of adults, as have the referenced rating scales developed by Drs. Barkley and Brown. The *DSM-IV* criteria for ADHD are listed in Chapter 3. A practical screening test for adult ADHD is the World Health Organization's Adult Self-Report Scale (ASRS), shown below. A positive score on this test has 80% specificity and 70% sensitivity for adult ADHD.

Adult Self-Report Scale*

Check the box that best describes how you have felt and conducted yourself over the past 6 months.

	Never	Rarely	Sometimes	Often	Very Often
1. How often do you have trouble wrapping up the final details of a project, once the challenging parts have been done?					
2. How often do you have difficulty getting things in order when you have to do a task that requires organization?					
3. How often do you have problems remembering appointments or obligations?					
4. When you have a task that requires a lot of thought, how often do you avoid or delay getting started?					
5. How often do you fidget or squirm with your hands or feet when you have to sit down for a long time?					
6. How often do you feel overly active and compelled to do things, like you were driven by a motor?					

Add the number of checkmarks that appear in the darkly shaded area. Four (4) or more checkmarks indicate that your symptoms may be consistent with Adult ADHD.

*Adapted from: Adult Self-Report Scale-Version1.1 (ASRS-V1.1) Screener by WHO (World Health Organization)

In addition to the essential history of hypomania and **ADHD**, most people with the COBAD syndrome have a history of depression. This may have been an episode of major depression, or of less severe chronic dysthymia. Some people have experienced *both* types of depression in their lives: chronic dysthymia with superimposed episodes of major depression, called "double depression." Finally, people with the COBAD syndrome have often experienced simultaneous symptoms of depression and hypomania, which is called a "bipolar mixed" state. As a matter of semantics, "mixed" bipolar states are supposed to be diagnosed only if a person has experienced full *mania*. My own view is that mixed states often occur in attenuated form in people who have been, at most, hypomanic. The *DSM-IV* criteria for major depression and dysthymia are listed in Chapter 2.

Most of my patients with the COBAD syndrome can recall episodes of depression in their childhood years, though few of them were diagnosed in childhood. Many have seen doctors and taken antidepressants at some time in their lives. It is helpful, diagnostically, to clarify the responses they have had to antidepressants. People with the COBAD syndrome, like those with bipolar disorders generally, have often had bad reactions to antidepressants. They often feel irritable and agitated (hypomanic), or notice a *rapid* improvement in their mood with worsening cycles of irritability and depression over time. Some COBAD syndrome adults in my practice have also felt *lethargic* on SSRI antidepressants, perhaps due to a down regulation of dopamine activity by SSRI's. I, personally, felt quite lethargic and "dull" on Prozac when I took it for six weeks in 1990, and felt much better after stopping it. (That is one reason why I never agreed with the "expert" recommendations by some psychiatrists and managed care companies that people who had failed to respond to a trial of an SSRI should be treated *next* with another SSRI, rather than with a different type of antidepressant.) It is not uncommon, in my experience, for people with the COBAD syndrome, like Roger and Carolyn, to present with symptoms of a mixed bipolar state *after being started on antidepressants*. They may feel depressed and suicidal with insomnia and agitation, irritability, or racing thoughts, a condition which may be quite dangerous due to the risk of suicide and impulsivity.

Finally, most of the COBAD syndrome adults that I have seen describe a history of anxiety problems. Almost all of them have experienced persistent generalized anxiety, and about half of my adult outpatients with the COBAD syndrome have experienced panic attacks. Many have also described anxiety problems in social settings, so-called "social phobia." My observations are consistent with the limited published research on comorbidity in bipolar children, and with the lone 2003 study of COBAD syndrome adults, by Dr. Biederman's group, showing that 75% of the childhood-onset bipolar *adults* had symptoms of two or more anxiety disorders. Like many of my COBAD syndrome patients, I have also experienced symptoms of social anxiety and atypical panic, probably caused by a genetic alteration of norepinephrine neurotransmission. As described in Dr. David Sheehan's classic monograph on panic disorder, *The Anxiety Disease*, people who have experienced panic attacks usually develop a conditioned response to situations in which panic has occurred. Consequently, they may suffer from generalized and "anticipatory" anxiety with a tendency to avoid situations, like crowded places or public speaking, in which they have experienced panic.

As a final clarification, it is important to emphasize that many *adults* with bipolar disorders, and many with ADHD, are *not* suffering from the COBAD syndrome. What does seem clear from the data is that *most children with bipolar disorders, probably 80-90%, have ADHD, the COBAD syndrome.* Conversely, in Dr. Biederman's research, only about 20-25% of children with *ADHD* met concurrent diagnostic criteria for a bipolar disorder. It is unclear what total percentage of children with ADHD eventually become bipolar. Some certainly do, because the data shows that about half of all teenagers who experience the onset of bipolar disorders *in adolescence* have comorbid ADHD. Unfortunately, epidemiological data about the incidence of ADHD in bipolar adults is, at present, scarce. I have seen a very high incidence of the COBAD syndrome in my bipolar II adult outpatients, but my private practice sample is far from representative of the general population, or of the population of adults with bipolar disorders. Many of my patients have seen multiple doctors, and have come to me because of persistent, treatment-resistant bipolar symptoms. Extrapolating loosely from Dr. Biederman's child data, which shows that 20-25% of children with ADHD have comorbid bipolar disorder, the COBAD syndrome could have an adult prevalence, in its more severe form, of more than 1%. As mentioned, I strongly suspect that its prevalence, in an *attenuated* form, is much higher in the general adult population.

Chapter 10

COBAD Syndrome II: Treatment Options

The COBAD syndrome, like ADHD and bipolar disorders generally, is a biologically based disorder, and most of the following discussion of treatment will focus on pharmacology. But it is important to emphasize that a number of non-pharmacological interventions may improve the course of the syndrome. Stress reduction, regular sleep, and exercise are important. Sobriety is also extremely important, though many people with untreated ADHD and bipolar disorders find it difficult to maintain sobriety. Research has shown that the use of stimulant medication in the treatment of ADHD can *reduce* the risk of substance abuse in affected individuals. This is important information, especially for people involved in Alcoholics Anonymous who may be understandably concerned about taking a prescription medication with abuse potential. Psychotherapy can play an important role in optimal recovery from ADHD and bipolar disorders, and should be integrated with adequate pharmacological treatment. Of all of these non-pharmacological interventions, I believe that *stress reduction* may be the most important. I have worked with bipolar patients over the years who could only achieve mood stability after quitting a stressful job or making other lifestyle changes to reduce stress: not commuting in heavy traffic, reducing debts, or leaving an abusive relationship. The best medications in the world will not work optimally if a person is experiencing chronic, unmitigated stress.

A great deal of research has been done during the past decade, and much has been written, about the treatment of bipolar disorders and ADHD. Unfortunately, there has been relatively little written about approaches to the treatment of *both disorders,* as seen in people with the COBAD syndrome. There are case studies from the child literature that have described successful treatment with combinations of mood stabilizers, stimulants, and the alpha-adrenergic agonist clonidine. The first *controlled* study on the treatment of children with the COBAD syndrome was published in January of 2005 in the *American Journal of Psychiatry* and involved the successful use of the mood stabilizer Depakote with the mixed amphetamine salt Adderall in a short-term trial. Depakote was used in this study because some data, especially one oft-quoted study by Dr. Charles Bowden, has shown that it may be more effective than lithium in the treatment of mixed bipolar states. The responses to lithium and Depakote monotherapy in some older studies of mixed bipolarity--summarized in a landmark review article by Dr. Susan McElroy in 1992--have ranged from 35% to 50%, respectively, though some of the pooled data was less than reliable. One recent retrospective study in adolescents with the COBAD syndrome showed no significant differences between lithium and Depakote in outcome. My own belief is that many people diagnosed in older studies with "mixed" bipolar states may have been suffering from the COBAD syndrome, with undiagnosed, untreated ADHD. Their poor responses to lithium and other mood stabilizers may have been due partly to untreated ADHD. Future controlled research looking at the prevalent, comorbid ADHD should help to clarify optimal approaches to the treatment of the COBAD syndrome in children and adults.

In this chapter I will present evidence from my own clinical experience, summarized in my March 2005 letter to the *American Journal of Psychiatry*, regarding effective treatment of adults with this syndrome. I would emphasize that *this approach should be used only with people who are reliable and able to keep the treating physician clearly informed of any problems that may arise during treatment.* There are significant risks associated with this approach that need to be carefully monitored. Conversely, there are significant risks associated with *not* adequately treating the full syndrome of disabling symptoms experienced by people with the COBAD syndrome. It is also important to emphasize that there may not be a single regimen that clearly works best for everyone suffering from the COBAD syndrome. Nevertheless, with time, patience, and perseverance, my patients and I have usually been able to find a regimen that controls both the mood disorder and the ADHD symptoms seen in the COBAD syndrome.

My approach always begins with mood stabilization. Because stimulant medications, which are the clear treatment of choice for ADHD, can induce hypomania and mood instability, I never start a stimulant in a bipolar patient without first achieving mood stabilization. But which mood stabilizer should be used? This has been an area of intense study in modern psychiatry, and the current large-scale Systematic Treatment Enhancement Program (STEP) studies, being conducted at multiple university settings in America, should help to clarify the relative efficacy of the treatment options. In recent years there has also been a great deal of research and advertising for the many new medications that have been shown to control *manic and mixed* bipolar symptoms, especially Depakote ER and the atypical antipsychotics: Risperdal, Zyprexa,

Geodon, Seroquel, and Abilify. This data should always be interpreted in light of private, for-profit marketing forces in modern "psychiatry."

My experience is that controlling mania or hypomania is not the most difficult task in the treatment of the COBAD syndrome, or of bipolar II disorders generally, although it is important, especially in the short-term when someone presents in a mixed bipolar state while taking an antidepressant. The more difficult, long-term problem is to treat and prevent *depression* without causing recurrences of hypomania or mood instability. Focusing on this central problem greatly simplifies the task of choosing a mood-stabilizing medication. In this regard, to date, there are four mood-stabilizing drugs that have been shown in placebo-controlled studies to improve the course of bipolar depression. They are *lithium, Lamictal, Zyprexa, and Seroquel*. Three other drugs, initially developed for the treatment of seizure disorders--Depakote, Tegretol, and Trileptal--may also be efficacious in the treatment of bipolar depression, and I do sometimes prescribe them for my patients, often in combination with lithium. Of the four best mood stabilizers for bipolar depression, three have also been found useful in the treatment of mania and mixed states: lithium, Zyprexa, and Seroquel. Lamictal may, at times, aggravate hypomanic symptoms, and I rarely use it as monotherapy, without concurrent use of another mood stabilizer. Seroquel, though useful, is often very sedating, especially at mood-stabilizing dosages, and Zyprexa often causes significant weight gain, hyperglycemia, and elevated serum cholesterol levels. So, what is left? *Lithium*, the good old-fashioned, inexpensive salt that I have been trying for years to convince my bipolar patients to take.

Unfortunately, lithium has a reputation as a "drug for crazy people that turns you into a zombie." I cannot tell you how many times I have heard this complaint from people for whom I have recommended a trial of lithium. A typical case was a young professional woman who came to see me several years ago after firing several psychiatrists. She sat down in my office and said: "I am *not* taking lithium!" At her insistence, we tried expensive new wonder drug after wonder drug before she finally, in desperation, agreed to try lithium several weeks later. The results were excellent. Within two weeks she felt much less depressed, less irritable, and was sleeping more soundly. I have prescribed lithium over the years for depressed bipolar patients who were sleeping sixteen hours per day and watched them wake up feeling more alert and less depressed within a few days. So much for becoming "zombies!" Some people do feel confused and "spacey" on lithium, especially at high doses, and when that happens I use a different mood stabilizer. I also try to use low doses of lithium, when possible, to reduce side effects. Many bipolar patients, in my experience, respond to fairly low doses. If they do not, I will then go "by the book" and increase the dose, as tolerated.

So, to return to the treatment of the COBAD syndrome, I usually start with lithium. If a person experiences persistent hypomanic symptoms on a therapeutic level of lithium, I have had best results adding Depakote ER, or low doses of the atypical antipsychotic Zyprexa, titrating the dose to control any residual hypomanic symptoms. Depakote, Zyprexa, and Seroquel are especially helpful for bipolar patients experiencing high anxiety (which, in my experience, is often aggravated by Risperdal and Geodon). However, if a person cannot tolerate them, due to weight gain, sedation, or metabolic disturbances, I will usually try Trileptal, the less toxic metabolite of Tegretol. I have also had success, on occasion, using other atypical antipsychotics such as Risperdal, Geodon, or Abilify. The combination of *Zyprexa and an SSRI antidepressant,* including the combination pill Symbyax, has also been dramatically effective for many of my treatment-resistant, depressed bipolar patients, although--judging from the most recent "expert guidelines"--the psychiatric experts have not realized this yet. Adding an SSRI to Zyprexa and/or lithium also often helps to control panic, social, and generalized anxiety disorders, which are frequently seen in the COBAD syndrome.

If a person remains depressed on the first-line mood stabilizer without hypomania, I often add Lamictal or an antidepressant to the regimen, though it is potentially dangerous to use Lamictal with Depakote due to a drug-drug interaction. (This is another reason why I usually begin with lithium rather than Depakote as a primary mood stabilizer.) I will also, at this point, consider starting a stimulant medication. Residual depression does often partially improve with the addition of stimulants. Let me emphasize, however, that *if hypomanic symptoms cannot be fully controlled in a stable, consistent manner, I never begin a trial of a stimulant medication.*

Once I have achieved mood stabilization with single or combination mood stabilizers, I move on to the next step and start a stimulant. I have had the best results using long-acting stimulants like Adderall XR and Ritalin LA, because the shorter half-life drugs tend to cause mood instability as they "wear off" periodically during the day. It is also often difficult for people with ADHD to remember to take the short half-life stimulants on schedule throughout the day. *Most of my COBAD syndrome patients have done best on the long-acting, mixed amphetamine salt Adderall XR,* while some have preferred Ritalin LA, especially those who have been overly activated on Adderall XR. I monitor carefully for signs of hypomania or psychosis after starting the stimulant, and stop them if such symptoms occur. Rather than becoming hypomanic, most of my COBAD syndrome patients feel *less agitated* and *less irritable* after starting stimulants. They also often feel less depressed and sleep more soundly, provided that they take the stimulant medication at the right time of day. Some, however, have not been able to tolerate stimulants and notice emergent hypomanic symptoms. This has been especially true of people suffering from more severe, bipolar type I disorders.

The following three case examples from my practice illustrate my treatment approach.

Case I

Donna, a 37-year-old administrative assistant, had been in treatment with me for several years. She had experienced recurrent episodes of depression and hypomania since childhood. Her mother was frequently hospitalized and treated with ECT during Donna's childhood, and a sister had suffered from mood swings and apparent psychosis since childhood years. Donna's mood had remained relatively euthymic for two years on Lithium, Lamictal, and low dose Risperdal, but she was functioning less than optimally in her daily activities. She described impaired concentration, increased social isolation, and a tendency to brood obsessively about a rude neighbor, which bordered on paranoia. She felt sedated and depressed on higher doses of Risperdal, but still anxious. After switching to low dose Zyprexa she felt less anxious and less depressed. I then discovered that she scored very highly on an ADHD symptom checklist, especially on the "inattentive" subscale. We tried Ritalin LA, then switched to Adderall XR. She felt markedly better on Adderall XR: not depressed or anxious, less irritable, and less worried

71

about her neighbor. Her total hours of sleep improved, and she did not experience subsequent hypomania.

Case 2

Monique, a 44-year-old interior designer, described a history of major depressive episodes since childhood years which had recurred after an initial positive response to Wellbutrin, prescribed by her primary care physician. On review, it was clear that she had also experienced episodes of hypomania throughout her life, though she had never been treated with mood stabilizers. She was in long-term remission from alcohol dependence. Her mother and two sisters were bipolar and alcohol dependent. Monique had a partial response to adding lithium to her Wellbutrin, but she remained moderately depressed and anxious. Her depression and anxiety improved with the addition of low dose Zyprexa. However, she described persistent difficulty organizing and concentrating on her work. We reviewed an ADHD symptom checklist, emphasizing symptoms since childhood years, and she scored very highly on scales of both inattention and hyperactivity. She noticed a marked improvement in her mood and concentration after starting Adderall XR. Her mood remained positive, without emergent hypomania, and she has made good use of psychotherapy to resolve a number of long-standing personal and professional problems.

Case 3

Phyllis, a 36-year-old sales manager, had been in treatment with me for several years following a hospitalization for severe depression and a suicide attempt. Her doctor had started her on Wellbutrin in the hospital and she felt much better after only one week. However, when I first saw her in my office two weeks later, she complained of insomnia, agitation, and extreme anxiety, characteristic of a mixed bipolar state. She had an allergic reaction to Depakote, then felt persistently depressed on Tegretol, so she was maintained on lithium and a low dose of Risperdal for two years, along with the anti-anxiety drug clonazepam to control episodic panic attacks. Lamictal was eventually added to prevent recurrent bouts of depression, but Phyllis continued to function very marginally in her work, and, ultimately, had to go on disability. After my discovery of Dr. Biederman's data on the COBAD syndrome, I realized that Phyllis had significant lifelong ADHD. I started her on Ritalin LA, and she and her family noticed a dramatic improvement in her anxiety, depression, and overall functioning. She achieved a stable remission of her ADHD symptoms--without emergent hypomania--on lithium, Lamictal, Risperdal, and Ritalin LA. She has had no panic attacks since starting Ritalin, and has looked like a completely different person during office visits: alert, calm, and able to engage in active conversations.

Chapter 11

COBAD Syndrome Families

As I began to systematically identify the COBAD syndrome in many of my adult patients, I also noticed that the syndrome could be recognized in many of their close *relatives*. This should have come as no surprise, since Dr. Biederman's group at Harvard had first identified early-onset bipolar disorder with ADHD as a familial syndrome almost ten years earlier. It was, for me, yet another example of the old medical adage, "You see what you look for." Janet, for example, a 54-year-old retired nurse, had been in treatment with me for several years. She had a clear history of the COBAD syndrome: chronic, recurrent depression with episodes of hypomania, and ADHD. Her mood had, ultimately, been stabilized on a regimen of lithium and Abilify, and her ADHD had been controlled with Ritalin LA. (She was one of my COBAD syndrome patients who had not been able to tolerate the more potent stimulant drug Adderall XR without becoming agitated and anxious.)

Janet came to a session one day with a request that I review a psychologist's report on her grandson, a ten-year-old who had been having problems at school. From the report it seemed likely that her grandson had ADHD. He was also depressed and anxious. Knowing Janet's history, and that many cases of childhood depression turn out to be early manifestations of bipolar disorders, I suspected that he was suffering from the COBAD syndrome. I suggested that Janet contact the boy's doctor about the family history of the COBAD syndrome, and that they consider adding Depakote or lithium to the regimen of stimulant medication that he was already taking. Unfortunately, I later found out that he was started on the SSRI antidepressant Zoloft without a mood stabilizer. He then started getting into fights on the playground and was suspended from school, probably after becoming hypomanic.

Another of my COBAD syndrome patients had a much more tragic story to tell. She was Sandra, a 26 year-old insurance agent who had been referred to me several years earlier for treatment of depression. She had been feeling despondent for several weeks after breaking up with her boyfriend, and was contemplating suicide. I was alarmed to learn that *both* her brother and a cousin had previously committed suicide. On review, she described feeling depressed and irritable since childhood years, though never *obviously* hypomanic. I suspected a bipolar type of depression, but started her on the SSRI antidepressant Paxil because she had done well on Paxil, prescribed by her family doctor, two years earlier. She did respond well to Paxil within one month, without any symptoms of hypomania, and continued to take it for the next twelve months. We then decided to continue the Paxil for a second year due to the chronicity and severity of her depressive symptoms prior to treatment. (Most people with chronic or recurrent depression need to remain on antidepressants for more than one year to prevent relapses.)

Sandra stopped the Paxil after two years, but became suicidally depressed a few months later. A friend, fortunately, insisted that she return to see me. She was reluctant to resume Paxil, because she thought it had caused weight gain, but did agree to try the new SSRI antidepressant Lexapro. Her mood improved on Lexapro, but she remained a bit sullen and, at times, irritable. She was also having great difficulty concentrating on classes at night school. As I reviewed her complaints about school I finally realized that Sandra had ADHD. We reviewed the adult symptom checklist, which confirmed an inattentive type of ADHD, and started Adderall XR. She then noticed a marked improvement in her concentration, and got A's on her examinations for the first time in her life that semester. Unfortunately, when she came to see me one month later, she appeared hypomanic. She was more talkative than usual and had been waking up early every morning, after only five hours of sleep, to take a demanding exercise class. As we carefully reviewed her history, it was apparent that she did, in fact, have a childhood-onset bipolar disorder with ADHD: the COBAD syndrome. Her father, a hard-working farmer, had always been driven and restless, rarely relaxing or sitting still. He had also been an alcoholic for many years. *Sandra's brother had impulsively committed suicide at age eighteen after feeling rejected by his girlfriend.* Her brother, like her father, had always been outgoing and energetic. Her father's family was vivacious, and several paternal relatives were alcoholics. A cousin, like Sandra's brother, had committed suicide in his youth.

I knew something about COBAD syndrome families because, like Sandra, I came from one. My siblings and I had all been fairly driven and hard working, but also prone to depression and irritability like my father. My sisters had grown up bickering with each other, and my brother and I could not play competitive sports without nearly killing each other: a problem that began when my father made us put on boxing gloves at an early age. My father, himself, was often depressed and irritable during my childhood: slamming doors, smashing plates, and routinely spanking my brother and me with a leather belt. For many years I had attributed his irritability to alcoholism and post-traumatic stress disorder (PTSD) from his combat experiences in World War II. He had served as an infantryman in a tank battalion that suffered heavy casualties during three years of combat. The war left him emotionally scarred and partially deaf. Although he rarely talked about his war experiences, he did write some stories and a memoir that I read after his death in 2004. I learned, at that time, that my father had been awarded a Bronze Star, and had once captured a contingent of Nazi soldiers at a forest encampment by himself. I also learned that he and his companions had slept in the rain and mud at Monte Casino for days while they were shelled, and often killed, by the German artillery on the high ground. Others later drowned during a tank maneuver in preparation for the invasion of the Rhone valley.

My father became an alcoholic during the war, like many combat veterans, and the problem persisted for years. But that was not the whole story. I realize now that he was probably hypomanic long before the war began. His mother told me that he would spend hours as a boy practicing his basketball shots and hitting golf balls, and he became an excellent basketball player and golfer. My mother recalls watching him win several high school basketball games with clutch shots at the buzzer, stories that were confirmed by two of my former patients who had played basketball with my father in high school and college. He also set many golf course records around the Denver area in his youth--shooting in the low 60's--and played in the U.S. Pro-Amateur tournament after the war. He once, apparently, won an improbable wager by playing eighteen holes of golf with only one club--a four iron--breaking par in the process.

I mention these details of my father's history because I believe that his intensity and drive may be typical of many people with the COBAD syndrome, and may be a peculiar feature of the disorder. One gets the impression from some of the academic papers on the subject that

77

children and adults with the COBAD syndrome are gravely disabled, almost sub-human. In reality, their drive and intensity may be highly adaptive to some extreme circumstances of human existence. Author Thom Hartman has written about the value of ADHD traits in hunter-gatherer cultures, and even in modern times. As an example, my father apparently surprised and captured a contingent of Nazi soldiers eating breakfast because he had, with his characteristic intensity, out-hiked the other men in his company on a hillside patrol. He approached dry fly fishing and golf with the same intensity, and had difficulty doing anything in moderation. He was like a car that had only two automatic gears: park and overdrive. With treatment, he might have been able to use the intermediate "gears" necessary for civilized life in the modern world.

Speaking from personal experience, I believe that it is extremely important for biological relatives of people with the COBAD syndrome to be carefully screened for the diagnostic features of the syndrome. This is also true, of course, for people with bipolar disorders or ADHD in general. Some of the warning signs and symptoms in a family member, as noted, are depression, irritability, impulsivity, chronic insomnia, substance abuse, and an impaired ability to complete detail-oriented work that is considered tedious. A moody child or adult who tends to hyperfocus when excited about something, then quits or fails to complete projects, should be carefully screened for ADHD and any history of hypomania. *People suffering from alcoholism should also be screened.* The proper diagnosis and treatment of the syndrome, at any age, is likely to have a substantial, positive impact on the health and welfare of many affected individuals and their families.

Chapter 12

COBAD Syndrome Children

I am not a child psychiatrist, but I have had ample experience dealing with my daughters, who both suffer from the COBAD syndrome. I have also become very familiar with the research literature on childhood bipolar disorders, in part, because my wife, Dr. Diane Lehman, is a child psychologist who has been actively involved in the Child and Adolescent Bipolar Foundation during the past several years. The most recent *Treatment Guidelines for Children and Adolescents with Bipolar Disorder,* sponsored by the Foundation, were published as I was writing this book in March of 2005, and they are consistent with my approach to treating the COBAD syndrome in adults, though they stop short of naming early-onset bipolar disorder with ADHD as an integral syndrome. They do emphasize the importance of diagnosing and treating comorbid ADHD, when possible, in bipolar children and adolescents.

Dr. Barbara Geller of Washington University has been in the forefront, along with Dr. Biederman's group at Harvard, in conducting research on early-onset bipolar disorders. Her book, *Bipolar Disorder in Childhood and Early Adolescence*, published in 2003, is an excellent review of the research literature on the subject. I had an opportunity to study a series of interviews with Dr. Geller that appeared in the journal *Affective Currents* recently. Among other things, she has been involved in the NIMH funded Treatment of Early-Age Mania (TEAM) studies. The TEAM approach to treating the COBAD syndrome in children parallels the approach that I have found most effective in treating my adult patients with this syndrome, although Dr. Geller has tended to avoid using Zyprexa due to the risk of weight gain and metabolic problems.

Dr. Joseph Biederman, together with his colleagues at Harvard, has played a central role for many years in identifying and studying the syndrome of bipolar disorder and ADHD in children. He and Dr. Janet Wozniak wrote a paper in 1996 describing their approach to treating the COBAD syndrome in children that has informed my own work with adults. Their continuing work will, no doubt, remain a gold standard for the ongoing diagnosis and treatment of the syndrome. A well written case report of a COBAD syndrome child was published by Drs. Rosanne State, Lori Altshuler, and Mark Frye in the *American Journal of Psychiatry* in June of 2002, and is worth reading carefully for its multi-faceted account of the clinical and family history, together with treatment responses. There have also been a series of case reports in recent years documenting the results of various medication trials in children with the COBAD syndrome that are consistent with the approach I have advocated in adults. Finally, the first controlled study of a mood stabilizer Depakote and the stimulant Adderall in the treatment of children with the COBAD syndrome was published in the January 2005 issue of the *American Journal of Psychiatry*. The results of the study were positive, and support the feasibility of using stimulants with mood stabilizers in children with the COBAD syndrome.

The treatment approach that I have advocated in this book for adults with the COBAD syndrome has also worked for my daughters, though my oldest daughter has been extremely sensitive to stimulant medication. It begins with mood stabilization, followed by titration of stimulants, as tolerated, to bring the ADHD into remission. Careful monitoring for emergent hypomania and psychosis is, of course, necessary, and there may be a subset of COBAD syndrome children, like some adults, who cannot tolerate stimulants without experiencing mood instability and psychosis. What is not acceptable, in my opinion, is for psychiatrists to focus only on treating the bipolar aspect of the disorder without *attempting* to treat the ADHD, if possible. The impaired executive functioning seen in ADHD can be gravely disabling throughout the life cycle, but seems particularly detrimental in childhood, when children need to acquire supportive friendships, self-esteem, and basic academic and social skills. Childhood peers can be cruel, and it is difficult enough for a *healthy* child to survive the slings and arrows of such imperious fortune. For the child with untreated ADHD, including those with the COBAD syndrome, it is next to impossible.

While the choice of an optimal mood stabilizer has not been clearly determined for bipolar children, most of my adult patients, and my own daughters, have experienced improved mood stability on lithium. A good case can also be made for Depakote, given the mixed and rapid-cycling nature of many childhood bipolar syndromes. (My own daughters were both, unfortunately, allergic to Depakote.) It was rated a "B&C" in the recent *Treatment Guidelines*, which rated Lithium an "A&B." Both of my daughters took Risperdal for more than one year, mainly on the basis of an early study done by retrospective chart review, from Dr. Biederman's group at the Massachusetts General, which showed that bipolar children responded better to Risperdal than to conventional mood stabilizers. They were also both experiencing psychotic symptoms which, according to Dr. Geller's data, are present in about 60% of bipolar children, and it seemed logical to use an antipsychotic drug that *also* appeared to work well as a mood stabilizer in childhood bipolar disorder.

Unfortunately, both of my daughters required very high doses of Risperdal to control their psychotic symptoms, and felt intermittently *depressed* and anxious on Risperdal. We noticed an overall improvement in their depression with the addition of lithium and, later, Lamictal. (Dr. Geller has advocated the use of lithium and/or Lamictal in depressed bipolar children, and has tended to use the older neuroleptic, chlorpromazine, in place of the newer atypical antipsychotics like Risperdal and Zyprexa, if needed.)

We eventually switched my daughters from Risperdal to *Zyprexa* and noticed that we were able to control their psychotic symptoms with far lower equivalent doses of Zyprexa. As I had seen with my adult patients, it appeared that Zyprexa was less "activating" than Risperdal (or Geodon, which we had tried briefly, without success, to control their psychotic symptoms on conventional doses). We also observed an overall improvement in their *generalized anxiety* on Zyprexa, although, as expected, they gained some weight after the switch. Abilify is emerging as a promising alternative to Zyprexa in bipolar maintenance, and does not cause the significant weight problems associated with Zyprexa. Unfortunately, it has not yet been shown in any controlled studies to improve bipolar *depression* as well as Zyprexa and Seroquel. Dr. Biederman's group published a controlled study showing that Abilify was effective for the treatment of childhood *mania* as I was completing this manuscript.

I should emphasize that the responses my daughters have had to treatment may not, necessarily, be generalized to other children with the COBAD syndrome. They are, however, consistent with the approach that has worked for many of my COBAD adult patients. We were able, after stabilizing their moods with a combination of lithium, Zyprexa, and

Lamictal, to improve their ADHD symptoms with the stimulant medication Adderall XR. The response was fairly dramatic, as I had often seen in my adult patients, and they were, if anything, less moody. My oldest daughter, to everyone's surprise, completed an entire fifth grade examination called the CSAP, required by Colorado State law, shortly after we started her on Adderall XR. A few days earlier, on the Saturday that she began taking Adderall XR, my youngest daughter, to my great surprise, challenged me to a game of "pig" basketball. She hadn't wanted to go outside for months, even to walk the dog, and I couldn't remember the last time she had wanted to play anything. She dribbled the ball around the court and won three games in a row with surprisingly good shooting. My aim was off, and I failed to make several key shots from three-point range behind her. It was the worst I had played since my medical school days at Harvard, but as I watched her play that day I felt more hopeful than I had felt in a long time.

Epilogue

I was excited when I realized, late in 2004, that the COBAD syndrome could be readily identified and successfully treated in many of my adult bipolar patients. There was little doubt in my mind that the proper identification and treatment of this syndrome in adults would be an important breakthrough in modern psychiatry. This conviction was the result of my many years of work with adults suffering from previously undiagnosed COBAD syndromes who had received "standard" psychiatric care for bipolar disorders. But how was I, a psychiatrist in private practice, to get the word out to the mental health community, and to the public? I wrote an article describing my clinical experiences diagnosing and treating adults with the syndrome and sent it to a few prominent psychiatrists and publishers, some of whom I had known during my years at Harvard or at the University of Colorado Health Sciences Center. My former residency director, Dr. Jay Scully, now the Medical Director of the American Psychiatric Association, suggested that I submit my article to the APA journal *Psychiatric Services*. Unfortunately, their editor told his assistant that what I had submitted was not "data," but only "speculation." Another editor, Dr. Alan Gelenberg of the *Journal of Clinical Psychiatry*, said, by way of his assistant, that he did not publish *clinical case material* from psychiatric practitioners at all, at least in article format. Dr. Joseph Biederman was kind enough to read my article, and suggested that I submit my findings as a condensed letter to the editor of a clinically oriented journal. Another distinguished professor I had known from my days at Harvard suggested that I might be able to publish my article in an obscure journal for psychiatric *practitioners* that I had never even heard of, much less read. It was hardly the major public health initiative that I thought necessary.

Ultimately, I submitted a condensed version of my article (shown in Chapter 8) as a letter to the editor of the *American Journal of Psychiatry* in March of 2005. Their letter editor, Dr. Jack Gorman, declined to publish it, as did Dr. Alan Gelenberg, the editor of the *Journal of Clinical Psychiatry*. One of Dr. Gelenberg's reviewers claimed that my "retrospective diagnoses of childhood ADHD in adults were probably not reliable." There were also comments that I did not include enough diagnostic and treatment details--despite the fact that I had been forced to condense the letter to a mere 500 words in order to have it considered for publication. I wrote to Dr. Gelenberg, pointing out that a study published in the *American Journal of Psychiatry* in 2000 had, in fact, shown that most adults *could* give reliable, accurate histories of their childhood ADHD symptoms, but I received no response. While I respected any legitimate editorial concerns about the reliability of published data, I was also frustrated. I knew that my findings were genuine, and that they had major public health implications, but I had not succeeded in convincing any academic psychiatrists that this was the case.

In fact, the only people who seemed to grasp the significance of my findings were a few psychiatrists in private practice from my old University Hospital call group. Like me, they had been treating bipolar adults for many years with the existing paradigms and practice standards. These standards had been endlessly promoted by CME (Continuing Medical Education) courses funded by pharmaceutical companies, and by articles in journals, like the *Journal of Clinical Psychiatry,* written by psychiatrists doing mostly short-term, placebo-controlled trials of new, expensive drugs for old paradigms. I had long known that many of the "expert guidelines" for the treatment of bipolar adults were inadequate in practice. Now I was learning firsthand *why* that was the case: *the people formulating America's psychiatric practice guidelines are not Emil Kraepelins.* They have not been carefully observing and treating patients in all of their complexity over the long term, noticing which diagnostic and treatment approaches work *well in practice*, and which do not. Instead, they have been reviewing checkmarks on lists of symptoms brought to them by research assistants. But there is no checkmark on the Hamilton Depression Scales or the Young Mania Rating Scales, used by research assistants in drug studies, to describe bipolar adults who suddenly feel "the best they have ever felt" in their lives--despite ten years of "standard" treatment--or the chronically depressed, irritable child who suddenly turns off the television set and wants to play basketball. Such data calls for more than the endorsement of yet another expensive drug to treat mania; it calls for a fundamental paradigm shift in our approach to diagnosing and treating many people with bipolar disorders.

Publishing this book proved no less daunting a task than publishing my article on the COBAD syndrome, for many of the same reasons. The publishers who responded to my queries, and those were few and far between, questioned my credentials and my claims about the COBAD syndrome. I was not a professor of psychiatry, or even a university employee. Why should they believe what I was writing about a psychiatric syndrome when others had not written about it? They were familiar with many of the popular books about ADHD and bipolar disorders written by reputable authorities that said nothing about a prevalent syndrome of childhood-onset bipolar disorder with ADHD in adults. I referred one such "acquisitions" editor to Dr. Barbara Geller's book *Bipolar Disorder in Childhood and Early Adolescence,* but he remained skeptical, especially when he learned that the editors of the *American Journal of Psychiatry* had refused to publish my findings.

I was up against two walls. The first has been experienced, I suspect, by anyone espousing a new paradigm. Most people, including physicians, publishers, and the general public, tend to readily embrace concepts that fit with an existing paradigm, even if the paradigm is inadequate. If the paradigm is questioned, they either fail to grasp what is being presented or they dismiss it as inconsistent with what they "know" to be true. No one, from the most closed-minded Biblical fundamentalist to the most sophisticated intellectual, wants to believe that his or her working model of reality is flawed. Yet, in the case of psychiatry, I have seen many widely accepted paradigms come and go, even during the past twenty years. The grandest of these has been the general paradigm shift from "interpretive," psychoanalytic models of some mental disorders to biologically based, "descriptive" models (and, hopefully, to a meaningful synthesis of the two). Lesser examples, described in this book, include changes in the paradigms, or dogmas, that ADHD does not exist in adults, that bipolar disorders do not exist in children, and that antidepressants should never be used in the treatment of bipolar disorders.

Another obstacle has to do with our cultural devaluation of psychiatry, and of mental health *practitioners*, in general. Psychiatry has long been devalued and stigmatized by the public, by the medical profession, and even by many administrative and academic psychiatrists. I have learned this during twenty years of work as a psychiatrist in a variety of settings, ranging from relatively posh private offices and hospitals to dilapidated state asylums, and even street corners in inner city barrios. There is, among other things, a widespread misconception that psychiatry is not a valid clinical *science,* with a knowledge and skill base requiring

87

careful study, training, and *practice*, just as people need to study and practice to become good internists or surgeons. Few people would seek an expert surgical opinion from a surgeon who had not performed an operation for years, but most "expert" opinions in American psychiatry are proffered by psychiatrists who have not treated patients for years, or even decades. Similarly, most people would not presume to tell a surgeon how to practice surgery, but there has rarely been a day in recent years when someone--usually a pharmaceutical company sales rep with "expert" opinions--has not tried to tell me how to practice psychiatry.

This devaluation of clinical psychiatrists is also due, in part, to our general fear and stigmatization of mental illnesses. Most people are disturbed by the notion that our thoughts, feelings, and actions--the essence of our *selves*--may not always be subject to our natural, voluntary control. Hence, if a person is depressed they are often told to "get over it," or, at most, to intervene in a voluntary or "natural" way: to exercise, meditate, or take a dietary supplement or herb, all of which may, of course, be helpful to some extent. There is a persistent cultural belief that we should not artificially remedy, or even label, disorders of the human brain in the same way that we remedy disorders of, for example, the eye. I can still remember the hand-painted billboards on a local highway in 1990--at the height of the Prozac scare--that said: "Psychiatry Kills!" And I suspect, fifteen years later, that if I had written a book claiming that bipolar disorders and ADHD are not "disorders" at all, or do not exist--much less co-exist--or can be effectively treated without medications, it *might* have been easier to find a publisher for my book.

In any case, as I complete this book, it is apparent to me that most psychiatrists who write the manuals and bestsellers have not yet made the paradigm shift toward conceptualizing the COBAD syndrome--childhood-onset bipolar disorder with ADHD and anxiety--as an *integral, inherited* disorder. I noticed, for example, that the "Benevian" family in Hallowell and Ratey's recently published bestseller, *Delivered From Distraction*, is clearly a COBAD syndrome family (on the wrong medications!) Most authors, like Drs. Hallowell and Ratey, are still writing about how to differentiate bipolar disorders *from* ADHD, and reviewing treatment approaches for the deconstructed syndromes of bipolar disorder *or* ADHD, in line with the early *DSM* tendency to diagnose primary, *exclusive* disorders. Even the most recent scholarly monographs and reviews on bipolar disorders that I have read--including Dr. Gary Sachs's 2004 monograph, *Managing Bipolar Affective Disorder*, and the preliminary Systematic Treatment Enhancement Program (STEP) publications in the *American Journal of Psychiatry*--have scarcely mentioned ADHD.

If this book accomplishes nothing else, then, it is my hope that it will lead to improved awareness, by psychiatrists and by the general public, that the syndrome I have described here--the COBAD syndrome--*is highly prevalent in our population, and that many people suffering from it are being inadequately treated as merely bipolar, or merely ADHD, with our current standards of psychiatric care.* I have learned this through my own personal, familial experience with this syndrome, and also as a psychiatrist who has tried for many years, with results that were often less than satisfactory, to provide effective treatment for patients with this previously unnamed syndrome. I wish that I could go back in time and have a second chance to treat them knowing what I know now! My only consolation in this regard is the hope that what I have learned and written about here will be helpful for many people who are likely to benefit from the proper diagnosis and treatment of the COBAD syndrome in the future. And for those affected by the COBAD syndrome, either personally or by its effects on their family members, my advice is to work closely and *patiently* with a psychiatrist who does not always pretend to have the right answers, but is always willing to ask the right questions, and to persevere in finding the right treatment for all aspects of the disorder.

References

Chapter 2

Akiskal, HS. (1995). Developmental pathways to bipolarity: are juvenile-onset depressions pre-bipolar? *J Am Acad Child Adolesc Psychiatry*, 34, 754-763.

Akiskal, HS, Maser, JD, Zeller, PJ, Endicott, J, Coryell, W, Keller, M, Warshaw, M, Clayton, P, & Goodwin, F. (1995). Switching from 'unipolar' to bipolar II: an 11-year prospective study of clinical and termperamental predictors in 559 patients. *Arch Gen Psychiatry*, 52, 114-123.

American Psychiatric Association (APA). (1994). *Diagnostic and statistical manual of mental disorders (4th ed)*. Washington, D.C.: American Psychiatric Association.

Bleuler, E. (1924). *Textbook of psychiatry*. New York: Macmillan.

Kraepelin, E.. (1962). *Lectures on clinical psychiatry*. New York: Hafner.

Winokur, G, Coryell, W, Endicott, J & Akiskal, H. (1993). Further distinctions between manic-depressive illness (bipolar disorder) and primary depressive disorder (unipolar depression). *Am J Psychiatary*, 150, 1176-1181.

Chapter 3

American Psychiatric Association (APA). (1994). *Diagnostic and statistical manual of mental disorders (4th ed)*. Washington, D.C.: American Psychiatric Association.

Barkley, RA. (1990). *Attention deficit hyperactivity disorder: a handbook for diagnosis and treatment*. New York: Guilford Press.

Biederman, J, Faraone, S, Keenan, KSV, Benjamin, J, Krifcher, B, Moore, C, Sprich-Buckminster, S, Ugaglia, K, Jellinek, MS, Steingard, R, et al. (1992). Further evidence for family-genetic risk factors in attention deficit hyperactivity disorder: patterns of comorbidity in probands and relatives in psychiatrically and pediatrically referred samples. *Arch Gen Psychiatry*, 49, 728-738.

Biederman, J, Mick, E, Faraone, SV, Braaten, E, Doyle, A, Spencer, T, Wilens, TE, Frazier, E & Johnson, MA. (2002). Influence of gender on attention deficit hyperactivity disorder in children referred to a psychiatric clinic. *Am J Psychiatary*, 159, 36-42.

Bush, G, Frazier, JA, Rauch, SL, Seidman, LJ, Whalen, PJ, Jenike, MA, Rosen, BR, & Biederman J. (1999). Anterior cingulate cortex dysfunction in attention-deficit/hyperactivity disorder revealed by fMRI and the Counting Stroop. *Biol Psychiatry*, 45, 1542-1552.

Dougherty, DD, Bonab, AA, Spencer, TJ, Rauch, SL, Madras, BK, & Fischman AJ. (1999). Dopamine transporter density in patients with attention deficit hyperactivity disorder. *Lancet*, 354, 2132-2133.

Dresel, S, Krause, J, Krause, KH, La Fougere, C, Brinkbaumer, K, Kung, HF, Hahn, K, & Tatsch, K. (2000). Attention deficit hyperactivity disorder: binding of [99mTc]TRODAT-1 to the dopamine transporter before and after methylphenidate treatment. *Eur J Nucl Med*, 27, 1518-1524.

Ernst, M, Liebenauer, LL, King, AC, Fitzgerald, GA, Cohen, RM, & Zametkin, AJ. (1994). Reduced brain metabolism in hyperactive girls. *J Am Acad Child Adolesc Psychiatry*, 33, 858-868.

Ernst, M, Zametkin, AJ, Matochik, JA, Pascualvaca, D, Jons, PH, & Cohen, RM. (1999). High midbrain [18F]DOPA accumulation in chidren with attention deficit hyperactivity disorder. *Am J Psychiatary*, 156, 1209-1215.

Faraone, SV, Doyle, AE, Mick, E, & Biederman, J. (2001). Meta-analysis of the association between the 7-repeat allele of the dopamine D(4) receptor gene and attention deficit hyperactivity disorder. *Am J Psychiatry*, 158, 1052-1057.

Goodman, R & Stevenson, J. (1989). A twin study of hyperactivity, II: the aetiological role of genes, family relationships and perinatal adversity. *J Child Psychol Psychiatry*, 30, 691-709.

La Hoste, GJ, Swanson, JM, Wigal, SB, Glabe, C, Wigal, T, King, N, & Kennedy, JL. (1996). Dopamine D4 receptor gene polymorphism is associated with attention deficit hyperactivity disorder. *Mol Psychiatry*, 1, 128-131.

MTA Cooperative Study Group. (1999). Fourteen-month randomized clinical trial of treatment strategies for attention deficit hyperactivity disorder. *Arch Gen Psychiatry*, 56, 1073-1086.

Wender, PH. (2001). *ADHD: attention-deficit hyperactivity disorder in children, adolescents, and adults.* New York: Oxford University Press.

Zametkin, AJ & Liotta, W. (1998). The neurobiology of attention-deficit/hyperactivity disorder. *J Clin Psychiatry*, 59 (Suppl 7), 17-23.

Zametkin, AJ & Rapoport, JL. (1987). Neurobiology of attention deficit disorder with hyperactivity: where have we come in 50 years? *J Am Acad Child Adolesc Psychiatry*, 26, 676-686.

Zametkin, AJ, Nordahl, TE, Gross, M, King, AC, Semple, WE, Rumsey, J, Hamburger, S & Cohen, RM. (1990). Cerebral glucose metabolism in adults with hyperactivity of childhood onset. *N Engl J Med*, 323, 1361-1366.

Chapter 4

Hallowell, EM & JJ Ratey. (1994). *Driven to distraction: recognizing and coping with attention deficit disorder from childhood through adulthood.* New York: Pantheon Books.

Chapter 5

Carlson, GA, Bromet, EJ & Sievers, S. (2000). Phenomenology and outcome of subjects with early- and adult-onset psychotic mania. *Am J Psychiatary,* 157, 213-219.

Faraone, SV, Biederman, J, Mennin, D, Wozniak, J, & Spencer, T. (1997). Attention-deficit hyperactivity disorder with bipolar disorder: a familial subtype? *J Am Acad Child Adolesc Psychiatry,* 36, 1378-1387.

Faraone, SV, Biederman, J, Wozniak, J, Mundy, E, Mennin, D, & O'Donnell, D. (1997). Is comorbidity with ADHD a marker for juvenile-onset mania? *J Am Acad Child Adolesc Psychiatry,* 36, 1046-4055.

Geller, B, Zimerman, B, Williams, M, DelBello, MP, Bolhofner, K, Craney, JL, Frazier, J, Beringer, L, & Nickelsburg, MJ. (2002). DSM-IV mania symptoms in a prepubertal and early adolescent bipolar disorder phenotype compared to attention-deficit hyperactive and normal controls. *Child Adolesc Psychopharmacol,,* 12, 11-25.

McElroy, SL, Altshuler, LL, Suppes, T, Keck, PE, Frye, MA, Denicoff, KD, Nolen, WA, Kupka, RW, Leverich, GS, Rochussen, JR, Rush, AJ, & Post, RM. (2001). Axis I psychiatric comorbidity and its relationship to historical illness variables in 288 patients with bipolar disorder. *Am J Psychiatary,* 158, 420-426.

Mick, E, Biederman, J, Faraone, SV, Murray, K & Wozniak, J. (2003). Defining a developmental subtype of bipolar disorder in a sample of nonreferred adults by age at onset. *J Am Acad Child Adolesc Psychiatry*, 13, 453-462.

Milberger, S, Biederman, J, Faraone, SV, Murphy, J, & Tsuang, MT. (1995). Attention deficit hyperactivity disorder and comorbid disorders: issues of overlapping symptoms. *Am J Psychiatry*, 152, 1793-1799.

Sachs, GS, Baldassano, CF, Truman, CJ & Guille, C. (2000). Comorbidity of attention deficit hyperactivity disorder with early- and late-onset bipolar disorder. *Am J Psychiatary*, 157, 466-468.

Schneck, CD, Miklowitz, DJ, Calabrese, JR, Allen, MH, Thomas, MR, Wisniewski, SR, Miyahara, S, Shelton, MD, Ketter, TA, Goldberg, JF, Bowden, CL, & Sachs, GS. (2004). Phenomenology of rapid-cycling bipolar disorder: data from the first 500 participants in the sytematic treatment enchancement program. *Am J Psychiatary*, 161, 1902-1908.

Schurhoff, F, Bellivier, F, Jouvent, R, Mouren-Simeoni, MC, Bouvard, M, Allilaire, JF & Leboyer, M. (2000). Early and late onset bipolar disorders: two different forms of manic-depressive illness? *Journal of Affective Disorders*, 58, 215-221.

Wozniak, J, Biederman, J, Kiely, K, Ablon, JS, Faraone, SV, Mundy, E, & Mennin, D. (1995). Mania-like symptoms suggestive of childhood-onset bipolar disorder in clinically referred children. *J Am Acad Child Adolesc Psychiatry*, 34, 867-876.

Chapter 6

Biederman, J, Baldessarini, RJ, Wright, V, Knee, D & Harmatz, JS. (1989). A double-blind placebo controlled study of desipramine in the treatment of ADD, I: efficacy. *J Am Acad Child Adoles Psychiatry*, 28, 777-784.

Hartmann, T. (2003). *Edison gene: ADHD and the gift of the hunter child.* Rochester, VT: Park Street Press.

Schildkraut, JJ. (1965). The catecholamine hypothesis of affective disorders: a review of supporting evidence. *Am J Psychiatry,* 122, 509-522.

Wilens, TE, Biederman, J, Prince, J, Spencer, TJ, Farone, SV, Warburton, R, Schleifer, D, Harding, M, Linehan, C, & Geller, D. (1996). Controlled study of desipramine for adult attention deficit hyperactivity disorder. *Am J Psychiatry,* 153, 1147-1153.

Chapter 7

Geller, B, Craney, JL, Bolhofner, K, Nickelsburg, MJ, Williams, M, & Zimerman, B. (2002). Two-year prospective follow-up of children with a prepubertal and early adolescent bipolar disorder phenotype. *Am J Psychiatary,* 159, 927-933.

Geller, B, Zimerman, B, Williams, M, Bolhofner, K & Craney, J. (2001). Bipolar disorder at prospective follow-up of adults who had prepubertal major depressive disorder. *Am J Psychiatary,* 158, 125-127.

Goldberg, JF, Harrow, M, & Grossman, LS. (1995). Course and outcome in bipolar affective disorder: a longitudinal follow-up study. *Am J Psychiatry,* 152, 379-384.

Keck, PE, McElroy, SL, Strakowski, SM, West, SA, Sax, KW, Hawkins, JM, Bourne, ML, & Haggard, P. (1998). 12-month outcome of patients with bipolar disorder following hospitalization for a manic or mixed episode. *Am J Psychiatary,* 155, 646-652.

Chapter 8

Altshuler, L, Suppes, T, Black, D, Nolen, WA, Keck, PE, Frye, MA, McElroy, S, Kupka, R, Grunze, H, Walden, J, Leverich, G, Denicoff, K, Luckenbaugh, D, & Post, R. (2003). Impact of antidepressant discontinuation after acute bipolar depression remission on rates of depressive relapse at 1-year follow-up. *Am J Psychiatry*, 160, 1252-1262.

Gijsman, HJ, Geddes, JR, Rendell, JM, Nolen, WA, & Goodwin, GM. (2004). Antidepressants for bipolar depression: a systematic review of randomized, controlled trials. *Am J Psychiatry*, 161, 1537-1547.

Scheffer, RE, Kowatch, RA, Carmody, T, & Rush, AJ. (2005). Randomized, placebo-controlled trial of mixed amphetamine salts for symptoms of comorbid ADHD in pediatric bipolar disorder after mood stabilization with divalproex sodium. *Am J Psychiatry*, 162, 58-64.

Chapter 9

Akiskal, HS. (1995). Developmental pathways to bipolarity: are juvenile-onset depressions pre-bipolar? *J Am Acad Child Adolesc Psychiatry*, 34, 754-763.

Brown, TE. (1996). *Brown attention-deficit disorders scales: manual.* San Antonio: Psychological Corp.

Connors, CK, Erhardt, D & Sparrow, EP. (1999). *Connors' adult ADHD rating scales: technical manual.* New York: Multi-Health Systems.

Hirschfeld, RMA, Williams, JBW, Spitzer, RL, Calabreses, JR, Flynn, L, Keck, PE, Lewis, L, McElroy, SL, Post, RM, Rapport, DJ, Russell, JM, Sachs, GS & Zajecka, J. (2000). Development and validation of a screening instrument for bipolar spectrum disorder: the mood disorder questionnaire. *Am J Psychiatry*, 157, 1873-1875.

McGough, JJ & Barkley, RA. (2004). Diagnostic controversies in adult attention deficit hyperactivity disorder. *Am J Psychiatry*, 161, 1948-1956.

Mick, E, Biederman, J, Faraone, SV, Murray, K & Wozniak, J. (2003). Defining a developmental subtype of bipolar disorder in a sample of nonreferred adults by age at onset. *J Am Acad Child Adolesc Psychiatry*, 13, 453-462.

Milberger, S, Biederman, J, Faraone, SV, Murphy, J, & Tsuang, MT. (1995). Attention deficit hyperactivity disorder and comorbid disorders: issues of overlapping symptoms. *Am J Psychiatry*, 152, 1793-1799.

Murphy, P & Schachar, R. (2000). Use of self-ratings in the assessment of symptoms of attention deficit hyperactivity disorder in adults. *Am J Psychiatary*, 157, 1156-1159.

Simon, NM, Otto, MW, Wisniewski, SR, Fossey, M, Sagduyu, K, Frank, E, Sachs, GS, Nierenberg, AA, Thase, ME & Pollack, MH. (2004). Anxiety disorder comorbidity in bipolar disorder patients: data from the first 500 participants in the systematic treatment enhancement program for bipolar disorder (STEP-BD). *Am J Psychiatry*, 161, 2222-2229.

Sheehan, D. (1983). *The anxiety disease.* New York: Scribner.

Wender, PH. (2001). *ADHD: Attention-deficit hyperactivity disorder in children, adolescents, and adults.* New York: Oxford University Press.

Chapter 10

Biederman, J, Wilens, T, Mick, E, Faraone, SV, Weber, W, Curtis, S, Thornell, A, Pfister, K, Jetton JG & Soriano, J. (1997). Is ADHD a risk factor for psychoactive substance use disorders? finding from a four-year prospective follow-up study. *J Am Acad Child Adolesc Psychiatry*, 36, 21-29.

Biederman, J, Wilens, T, Mick, E, Milberger, S, Spencer, TJ & Faraone, SV. (1995). Psychoactive substance use disorders in adults with attention deficit hyperactivity disorder (ADHD): effects of ADHD and psychiatric comorbidity. *Am J Psychiatry*, 152, 1652-1658.

Bowden, CL. (2000). The ability of lithium and other mood stabilizers to decrease suicide risk and prevent relapse. *Current Psychiatry Reports*, 2, 490-494.

Bowden, CL, Brugger, AM, Swann, AC, Calabrese, JR, Janicak, PG, Petty, F, Dilsaver, SC, Davis, JM, Rush, AJ, Small, JG, Garza-Trevino, ES, Risch, SC, Goodnick, PJ & Morris, DD. (1994). Efficacy of divalproex vs lithium and placebo in the treatment of mania. *JAMA*, 271, 918-924.

Kafantaris, V. (1995). Treatment of bipolar disorder in children and adolescents. *J Am Acad Child Adolesc Psychiatry*, 34, 732-741.

McElroy, SL, Keck, PE, Pope, HG, Hudson, JI, Faedda, GL & Swann, AC. (1992). Clinical and research implications of the diagnosis of dysphoric or mixed mania or hypomania. *Am J Psychiatry*, 149, 1633-1644.

Sachs, G. (2004). *Managing bipolar affective disorder*. London: Science Press Ltd.

Scheffer, RE, Kowatch, RA, Carmody, T, & Rush, AJ. (2005). Randomized, placebo-controlled trial of mixed amphetamine salts for symptoms of comorbid ADHD in pediatric bipolar disorder after mood stabilization with divalproex sodium. *Am J Psychiatry*, 162, 58-64.

State, RC, Altshuler, LL, & Frye, MA. (2002). Mania and attention deficit hyperactivity disorder in a prepubertal child: diagnostic and treatment challenges. *Am J Psychiatry*, 159, 918-925.

State, RC, Frye, MA, Altshuler, LL, Strober, M, DeAntonio, M, Hwang, S, & Mintz, J. (2004). Chart review of the impact of attention-deficit/hyperactivity disorder comorbidity on response to lithium or divalproex sodium in adolescent mania. *J Clin Psychiatry*, 65, 1057-1063.

Wozniak, J & Biederman, J. (1996). A pharmacological approach to the quagmire of comorbidity in juvenile mania. *J Am Acad Child Adolesc Psychiatry*, 35, 826-828.

Chapter 11

Biederman, J. (2003). Pharmacotherapy for attention-deficit/hyperactivity disorder (ADHD) decreases the risk for substance abuse: findings from a longitudinal follow-up of youths with and without ADHD. *J Clin Psychiatry*, 64 (Suppl 11), 3-8.

Biederman, J, Wilens, T, Mick, E, Faraone, SV, Weber, W, Curtis, S, Thornell, A, Pfister, K, Jetton JG & Soriano, J. (1997). Is ADHD a risk factor for psychoactive substance use disorders? finding from a four-year prospective follow-up study. *J Am Acad Child Adolesc Psychiatry*, 36, 21-29.

Faraone, SV, Biederman, J, Mennin, D, Wozniak, J, & Spencer, T. (1997). Attention-deficit hyperactivity disorder with bipolar disorder: a familial subtype? *J Am Acad Child Adolesc Psychiatry*, 36, 1378-1387.

Hartmann, T. (2003). *Edison gene: ADHD and the gift of the hunter child*. Rochester, VT: Park Street Press.

Chapter 12

Biederman, J, McDonnell, MA, Wozniak, J, Spencer, T, Aleardi, M, Falzone, R, & Mick, E. (2005). Aripiprazole in the treatment of pediatric bipolar disorder: a systematic chart review. *CNS Spectr*, 10, 141-148.

Frazier, JA, Meyer, MC, Biederman, J, Wozniak, J, Wilens, TE, Spencer, TJ, Kim, GS & Shapiro, S. (1999). Risperidone treatment for juvenile bipolar disorder: a retrospective chart review. *J Am Acad Child Adolesc Psychiatry*, 38, 960-965.

Geller, B & MP DelBello (Eds.). (2003). *Bipolar disorder in childhood and early adolescence.* New York: Guilford.

Kafantaris, V. (1995). Treatment of bipolar disorder in children and adolescents *J Am Acad Child Adolesc Psychiatry*, 34, 732-741.

Kowatch, RA, Fristad, M, Birmaher, B, Wagner, KD, Findling, RL, Hellander, M, & the Workgroup Members. (2005). Treatment guidelines for children and adolescents with bipolar disorder: child psychiatric workgroup on bipolar disorder. *J Am Acad Child Adolesc Psychiatry*, 44, 213-235.

Rosenblatt, JE & NC Rosenblatt. (2004). Assessment and management of pediatric bipolar disorder and unipolar depression (part I of an interview with Barbara Geller, MD). *Currents in Affective Illness*, 23, 5-11.

Rosenblatt, JE & NC Rosenblatt. (2005). Assessment and management of pediatric bipolar disorder and unipolar depression (part II of an interview with Barbara Geller, MD). *Currents in Affective Illness*, 24, 5-13.

Scheffer, RE, Kowatch, RA, Carmody, T, & Rush, AJ. (2005). Randomized, placebo-controlled trial of mixed amphetamine salts for symptoms of comorbid ADHD in pediatric bipolar disorder after mood stabilization with divalproex sodium. *Am J Psychiatry*, 162, 58-64.

State, RC, Altshuler, LL, & Frye, MA. (2002). Mania and attention deficit hyperactivity disorder in a prepubertal child: diagnostic and treatment challenges. *Am J Psychiatary*, 159, 918-925.

Wozniak, J & Biederman, J. (1996). A pharmacological approach to the quagmire of comorbidity in juvenile mania. *J Am Acad Child Adolesc Psychiatry*, 35, 826-828.

Epilogue

Geller, B & MP DelBello (Eds.). (2003). *Bipolar disorder in childhood and early adolescence.* New York: Guilford.

Hallowell, EM & JJ Ratey. (2005). *Delivered from distraction: getting the most out of life with attention deficit disorder.* New York: Ballantine Books.

Sachs, G. (2004). *Managing bipolar affective disorder.* London: Science Press.

Suggested Reading

Barkley, RA. (2000). *Taking charge of ADHD: the complete, authoritative guide for parents.* New York: Guilford.

Birmaher, B. (2004). *New hope for children and teens with bipolar disorder.* New York: Three Rivers Press.

Fawcett, J, Golden, B & N Rosenfeld. (2000). *New hope for people with bipolar disorder.* Roseville, CA: Prima Health.

Geller, B & MP DelBello (Eds.). (2003). *Bipolar disorder in childhood and early adolescence.* New York: Guilford.

Goodwin, FK & KR Jamison. (1990). *Manic-depressive illness.* Oxford: Oxford Press.

Green, RW. (1998). *The explosive child: a new approach for understanding and parenting easily frustrated, chronically inflexible children.* New York: HarperCollins.

Hallowell, EM & JJ Ratey. (1994). *Driven to distraction: recognizing and coping with attention deficit disorder from childhood through adulthood.* New York: Pantheon Books.

Hallowell, EM & JJ Ratey. (2005). *Delivered from distraction: getting the most out of life with attention deficit disorder.* New York: Ballantine Books.

Hartmann, T. (2003). *Edison gene: ADHD and the gift of the hunter child.* Rochester, VT: Park Street Press.

Jamison, KR. (2004). *Exuberance: the passion for life.* New York: Knopf.

Jamison, KR. (1993). *Touched with fire: manic-depressive illness and the artistic temperament.* New York: Maxwell Macmillan International.

Miklowitz, DJ. (2002). *The bipolar disorder survival guide: what you and your family need to know.* New York: Guilford.

Nadeau, KG, Quinn, PO, Littman, E & P Quinn. (2000). *Understanding girls with attention deficit hyperactivity disorder.* Longwood, FL: Advantage Books.

Papolos, DF & J Papolos. (1999). *The bipolar child.* New York: Broadway Books.

Sachs, G. (2004). *Managing bipolar affective disorder.* London: Science Press.

Sheehan, D. (1983) *The anxiety disease.* New York: Scribner.

Weiss, M, Hechtman, LT, & G Weiss. (1999). *ADHD in adulthood: a guide to current theory, diagnosis, and treatment.* Baltimore: The Johns Hopkins University Press.

Wender, PH. (2001). *ADHD: Attention-deficit hyperactivity disorder in children, adolescents, and adults.* New York: Oxford University Press.

Wilens, TE. (1999). *Straight talk about psychiatric medications for kids.* New York: Guilford.

Index

D

DAT, 22

Depakote (valproic acid), 28, 50-51, 66-70, 73-74, 80-81

depression, 8, 10-11, 13-15, 24, 26-28, 30, 32, 37-39, 47, 50, 52, 54, 57, 58, 62, 68, 70-78, 82, 91, 97, 101

desipramine, 5, 21, 38-42, 44, 95-96

dopamine, 20, 22, 47, 62, 92-93

receptors, 22

Driven to Distraction, 30, 94, 103

dysthymia, 11, 14, 39, 62

E

EEG (qEEG), 21

F

Faraone, Stephen, 56, 92-95, 98-100

G

Geller, Barbara, 32, 79, 80-82, 86, 94, 101-103

generalized anxiety, 45, 48, 63, 70, 82

Geodon, (ziprasidone), 67, 69, 82

Goodwin, Frederick, 56, 91, 97, 103

H

hyperfocusing, 43, 47, 78

hyperthymic temperament, 11

hypomania, 5, 11-12, 15-16, 18-19, 41, 47, 49, 50-53, 55-58, 60, 62, 67-75, 78, 81, 99

I

irritability, 5, 11, 27, 32, 39, 47, 56, 60, 62-63, 76, 78

K

Kraepelin, Emil 8-11, 24, 91

L

Lamictal (lamotrigine), 68, 70-71, 73, 82-83

Lexapro (escitalopram), 14, 28, 38, 50, 75

lithium, 10, 15, 28, 30, 50-51, 55, 66, 68-70, 72-74, 81-82, 99-100

Luvox (fluvoxamine), 14, 28, 38, 50, 75

M

mania, 5, 8, 10-11, 15, 19, 32, 55-56, 58-60, 62, 67-68, 82, 86, 94, 99-100, 102

Milberger, Sharon, 56, 95, 98-99

Printed in the United States
53944LVS00004B/421

9 781420 867015